NOT DEAD YET

WHAT FUTURE FOR LABOR?

MARK LATHAM

Black Inc.

Published by Black Inc.,
an imprint of Schwartz Media Pty Ltd
37–39 Langridge Street
Collingwood VIC 3066 Australia
email: enquiries@blackincbooks.com
http://www.blackincbooks.com

The National Library of Australia Cataloguing-in-Publication entry:

    Latham, Mark, 1961- author.

    Not dead yet : what future for Labor? / Mark Latham.

    ISBN: 9781863956215 (paperback)

    Australian Labor Party.
    Politicians--Australia. Conservatism--Australia.
    Australia--Politics and government--2001-

    324.29407092

Printed in Australia by Griffin Press an Accredited ISO AS/ NZS 14001:2004
Environmental Management System printer.

CONTENTS

NOT DEAD YET

INTRODUCTION

In May 2012 something unusual happened. A Labor factional powerbroker said something positive about me. Speaking at the National Press Club in Canberra, the high-profile secretary of the Australian Workers' Union, Paul Howes, suggested it was time to end the mutual hostility between the party and myself.

"Maybe the time's come to stop being so particular about particular leaders or former leaders, constantly spending so much air-time ripping into ourselves," he said. "I'm as guilty of this as anyone else. The time has come for our movement to be more tolerant of dissent, to be more tolerant of diversity, to bring back those lost members, those cousins who don't come to Christmas anymore."

My last Christmas dinner with the ALP was in 2004. Four weeks later I resigned as the federal leader of the party and as the Member for Werriwa. My motivations were many: overcoming ill-health, ending the torment of time away from family, detesting large sections of the media and disenchantment with Labor's union-based factional system. Thereafter, I allowed my ALP membership ticket to lapse, ending my 25-year involvement in party politics. I became a rare breed – having resigned from parliament for "family reasons" I actually spent more time with my family, becoming the primary carer of my children.

In September 2005 I published my diaries, a frank account of life inside the Labor family. This ensured a long absence from future Christmas festivities. I was portrayed as a Grinch-like figure, the man who tried to steal Labor's credibility. The initial reaction to my book was one of denial and denigration. With only a few dissenters, Australia's political class united in declaring my critique to be absurd. To paraphrase the words of many: "The Labor Party can't be as bad as that; the bastard has gone mad."

This remained the orthodoxy until the beginning of 2010. Then something changed. People who had once looked the other way in the shopping aisles at Woolworths began to greet me like a long-lost friend, exclaiming, "Gee, you were right about Rudd in that book of yours." Labor Party members I had once known contacted me, expressing regret that they had not taken my views seriously and we had not stayed in touch.

Some media commentators even altered their stance, acknowledging that many of the party's problems, especially in its organisational roots, had been foreshadowed in *The Latham Diaries*. The federal caucus was as bad as my book had said – a harbinger to the chaos of Labor in government. I had told the truth about the party's internal condition but, as often happens in public life, it took many years for the truth to be accepted. At this point, again in the spirit of Christmas dinner, I could have joined with Noël Coward in declaring, "Legitimate at last. Won't Mother be pleased?"

Labor's membership crisis

During the terms of the Rudd and Gillard governments, criticism of the ALP has become something of a national pastime. The processes of government have resulted in greater transparency about the true state of the Labor movement. The ALP's rank-and-file membership has collapsed, concentrating power in an oligarchy of union-based factional leaders. Active trade unionism has also declined, with the Health Services Union scandal revealing a culture of nepotism and financial abuse.

The two problems are linked. Union numbers at Labor conferences have conferred factional power on a relatively small number of union chiefs. This factional control, in turn, has spawned arrogance – the type of conceit by which union officials assume that union money is their money. The countervailing influence of broad-based party and trade union membership, the traditional ballast of the Labor movement, has been lost.

Unionisation in Australia has fallen to 18 per cent economy-wide, with private sector coverage at just 13 per cent. Whether the traditionalists like it or not, minority union membership is here to stay. In a highly skilled and competitive modern economy – dominated by small businesses, contractors and information workers – it is impossible to organise mass union membership. A majority of economic agents see no need for collective representation. They have the qualifications and confidence to bargain effectively on their own behalf.

The problem for Labor, with its concentrated base of

union affiliations and financing, lies in the organisational imbalance between the new economy and old-style unionism. In the workforce, unions have become a minority influence, whereas inside the ALP, through the strength of the factional system, they have maintained a majority complex, exercising control over party decision-making.

Having watched their relevance in the workplace fade over the past thirty years, union officials have compensated by beefing up their role inside the Labor Party. In practice in Australia, there is no longer any such thing as a powerful unionist, as expressed by the traditional notion of industrial leverage. There is, however, a generation of union leaders who have made themselves powerful by using their union's resources to exercise factional influence inside the ALP. This has been a classic "big fish in a small pond" strategy.

It has been made easier by the long-term decline in Labor branch membership. In any organisation, power flows to the centre whenever a critical mass of grassroots participation is lost. This concentration of influence usually results in self-serving processes and decisions, generating ethical problems and further disillusionment among rank-and-file members. In this fashion, oligarchies feature a vicious circle of centralised power and membership decline. Over time, the preservation of power internally is regarded as a higher priority than satisfying the organisation's external goals.

The formalisation of Labor's factional system in the 1980s has coincided with a hollowing out of party membership. The Labor historian Troy Bramston has chronicled the collapse: from 150,000 members nationally in the 1930s, to 50,000 in the 1990s, to just 11,665 members who voted in the ballot for the ALP national presidency in November 2011. In many parts of the nation, branches which once flourished as forums of working-class activism and community participation have closed down. At each election, the party has had to rely on a dwindling number of volunteers to distribute its literature and staff its polling booths.

The problem is particularly acute in outer-suburban areas – the key marginal seats Labor needs to win to hold government. As the strength of union-based factionalism has increased, party members have lost interest in local branch meetings. Young families and professional people, already burdened by long commuting journeys and lifestyle pressures, have had no reason to maintain their involvement.

Compared to rival community organisations, the return on ALP membership is minimal. Active branch life has been reduced to a hard core of the ageing party faithful, plus members of parliament and their staff and other hustling aspirants for elected office. On the rollcall of inactive members, ethnic branch-stacking, while not as bad as in the 1990s, remains a problem.

In effect, Labor has split into two organisations, each operating in a different sphere of political activity. Branches go through the motions of monthly meetings and debate, knowing that their resolutions will be ignored by the party hierarchy. Their members blame the factional system for ruining the traditional Labor ethos of rank-and-file participation. This is the politics of permanent complaint at a local level.

At the party's centre, the branches are viewed as an irritation, a mid–twentieth century anachronism. Factional leaders rarely attend party meetings in their local electorate, looking down their noses at the tedium and irrelevance of such gatherings. In the exercise of their power, this is not an irrational outlook. Why bother with the party's grassroots, huddled together in dank community halls, when the union/factional bosses can make real decisions, wielding influence around the lunch tables of inner-city restaurants?

When we think of Labor Party splits, the parliamentary schisms of 1916, 1931 and 1955 come to mind – in each case, highlighted by the decision of a significant proportion of Labor MPs to leave the party. The current split is different and, in many respects, more serious. The union/factional wing of the party has divorced itself from the rank and file.

Thus modern Labor is living an institutionalised fallacy. It is two parties in one, two divisions pulling against each other. The ALP historian and former NSW minister Rodney Cavalier has spoken of the "party below" (its disenfranchised membership), the corollary of which is the "party above" (its dominant powerbrokers). These two organisations have little in common, beyond the name "Labor" and a romantic attachment to the notion of working-class struggle.

The ALP's original purpose, the mass participation of working men and women in parliamentary democracy, has dissolved. Very few unionists are still active in the party below. This is clear from statistics released by the former NSW assistant general secretary Luke Foley. Only 16 per cent of party members belong to a trade union affiliated to the ALP. By far the biggest category (55 per cent) is concessional membership, that is, people outside the workforce, mainly retirees.

When extrapolated to the 2011 national presidency vote, Foley's figures expose the emptiness of Labor's structure. Of the party's 11,665 members participating in the ballot, only 1860 (16 per cent of the total) were likely to belong to a Labor-affiliated union. This represents, on average, just twelve trade unionists in each federal electorate – not enough for a rugby team.

As a party of working-class activism, Labor now resembles a Hollywood back lot. There's nothing behind the facade. Walk through the doors of the main-street saloon and you find yourself wandering around an empty carpark. Grassroots union activism in Australia has ended and, with it, the energy which once powered political Labor has faded. As Cavalier has recorded:

> Contested union ballots, like attendances at union meetings, reveal how very few members take the slightest interest in the affairs of their unions. The proportion of members of affiliated unions who belong to the ALP is fewer than 0.5 per cent. Belonging to the ALP is not part of the life of a modern Australian worker.

In organising Labor Party numbers, it is many decades since union officials tried to recruit unionists into the local branches. Union power is now exercised through centralised control: union secretaries donating money and staff to marginal seats and rounding up the numbers at state and federal Labor conferences. The grand old party of working-class participation has become a virtual party, top-heavy with union/factional bosses.

In no other part of society – whether in the corporate sector, community groups or government agencies – could an organisation function this way and expect to survive. This is the core delusion of 21st-century democracy, that political parties can fragment and hollow out, yet still win the confidence of the people.

For a party of reform like Labor, the condition is doubly debilitating. Social change needs to be a bottom-up process, with reformers drawing ideas from the community, testing those ideas at a local level and using them in the development of national policy. Labor has always been strongest when it has followed this technique: advancing a reform agenda but not getting too far ahead of public opinion.

Rediscovering this process in an era of widespread public disengagement from party politics is a difficult task, but one essential to Labor's future. It is the key to effective organisational reform. Otherwise the party will continue to shrivel into a dispirited back lot, living off the glories of the past but unable to attract and inspire the next generation of social reformers.

Labor's identity crisis

The corrosion of Labor's culture has produced a crisis of Labor identity. The party is confused on economic policy, not knowing whether to embrace the Keating legacy of micro-reform and productivity growth or to accede to the sectional demands of union/factional bosses and the anti-competitive comfort of industry welfare.

As union coverage tends to be highest in old, declining industries, such as smokestack manufacturing, the demand for protection and subsidisation is disproportionately strong inside the Labor movement. This is at odds with Keating's creation of a "miracle economy," delivering twenty years of uninterrupted growth and wealth creation through the liberalisation of economic policy.

The union oligarchy is also at odds with the rise of Australia's new aspirational class: the free agents of the new economy (the start-up entrepreneurs, contractors and information-rich specialists) who resent the intervention of outsiders, whether in the form of excessive government regulation or trade union collectivism. This is a problem not just in economic management, but also the development of social policy. Given a choice between traditional left thinking – reflected in the paternalism of welfare-state programs – and the aspirational demand for individual entitlements and flexibility, Labor still sides with the former.

In combination these problems have damaged the party's electoral standing. The aspirational class is the fastest growing part of the electorate, yet much of the ALP's policy-making is still directed towards a declining working-class constituency. The underlying voting trends in recent years have been alarming.

Generations of Australians who grew up with the assumption of an evenly balanced two-party system have had to recast their thinking. In March 2011 the Labor primary vote at the NSW election fell below 25 per cent – a figure more befitting an interest group than a mainstream party. Twelve months later in Queensland, Labor's parliamentary representation was reduced to the size of a netball team. In these two states, the longevity of the outgoing ALP governments was a factor.

There is no such excuse for the way in which the party was routed in September's federal election. A government just two terms old, led by someone the caucus had deemed to be its best campaigner and most popular personality, lost seventeen seats, mostly along the eastern seaboard. The Rudd government's primary vote of 33.4 per cent was the party's worst performance in seventy-nine years, since the leadership of Jim Scullin in the 1930s. In traditional heartland regions like Western Sydney, most of the seats are now either Liberal-held or highly marginal for the ALP.

Optimists argue this is a cyclical phenomenon, that Labor will rebound once the high-water mark of Liberal dominance in Australia is reached. If only politics were like the world's oceans, with the tides of electoral support moving with metronomic precision. The party's bigger problem is structural, the steady erosion of its traditional working-class base. Across the suburban flatlands of Australia's major cities, people who grew up in fibro shacks now live in solid-stone double-storey affluence. Families which were once resigned to a lifetime of blue-collar work now expect their children to be well-educated professionals and entrepreneurs.

Seats in Sydney's west have swung against Labor because, in their economic base and prosperity, they are now little different to other parts of the country. Rising income levels have transformed the electoral map. Whenever I drive through the region, I am struck by the ongoing emergence of new middle-class suburbs. The electoral pendulum is moving 1–2 per cent against Labor each parliamentary term, solely by the weight of demographic and economic change. No matter the quality and tenacity of local members, the tide is going out on the party.

In this respect, the Labor movement is a victim of its own success. With their economic reforms the Hawke and Keating governments freed up social mobility, ending the rigidity of Australia's class structure. A deregulated economy has given workers the chance to gain access to capital and establish small businesses. This is a tremendous force for growth and wealth accumulation, making it the greatest economic achievement of Labor's history in government. Politically, however, it has cannibalised a large portion of the party's base. The working class has gone the way of record players and typewriters – a social relic irrelevant to the future shape of the Labor movement.

As a party dedicated to achieving a democratic majority, the ALP cannot win office and exercise power without the support of the rising aspirationals. This makes its egalitarian goals doubly difficult. The new grouping commands an electoral influence which cannot be ignored. Yet the pressing social justice issue in Australia is to address the problems of an entrenched underclass – people who have missed out on economic mobility, who are seemingly excluded from all forms of employment and social ambition.

The problem for this group is not the adequacy of income support. The Australian welfare system is generous enough for recipients to cover basic living costs. Indeed, since the mid-1980s, people on government benefits have experienced an increase in real disposable income of 11.9 per cent. Rather, the entrenchment of poverty comes primarily from social factors: disadvantaged people living in disadvantaged places, with an absence of effective role models and behavioural norms. In practice, this group has gone feral, leading lives of welfare dependency, substance abuse and street crime. Their political influence is minimal: many are not on the electoral roll and those who are tend to live in safer Labor seats.

As the working class has splintered, most of Labor's constituency has climbed upwards in society, while a residual cohort has fallen back. In its values and policies, the ALP needs to straddle these two groupings, in a political setting in which its membership base and the viability of trade unionism are in decline. So far, the party is yet to overcome the Biblical challenge of serving two masters. It has not won the political trust of the new aspirational class, nor has it found new ways of solving the slow-burning crisis of the underclass.

A third splintering force has made the reform task even harder: the rise of climate change as the pre-eminent environmental issue of our time. In a labour-based party, there is a sharp tension between union officials whose members work in carbon-intensive industries and Labor MPs who recognise the dangers of global warming and the need for collective action. This conflict has been evident in ALP policy-making since 2006. Senior unionists have wanted the party to soft-pedal on this issue, while the parliamentary Left faction has urged a more aggressive stance.

Adding to this difficulty is the electoral task of selling climate change policies to aspirational voters in marginal seats. The new economic class has a strong focus on consumerism. This is a natural consequence of its financial success. Its favourite recreational activity is shopping. While it has little problem with other people making economic sacrifices to reduce the nation's carbon footprint, it does not respond well to the idea of individual sacrifice.

This contradiction, more than any area of policy, destroyed Kevin Rudd's first term as prime minister. He was elected in 2007 on a promise of addressing the cost-of-living pressures on "working families," yet he also hailed climate change as the "great moral challenge of our generation." Logically, the most effective way of reducing carbon consumption in a market economy is to increase its price – a strategy in direct defiance of the government's living-standards mantra. In early 2010, Rudd conceded defeat in reconciling these goals. He accepted the poll-driven advice of party officials to shelve his Emissions Trading Scheme. Not surprisingly, policy chaos and broken promises followed – a position from which Labor is yet to recover.

Later in this essay, I argue the case for the party maintaining a high-profile campaign on the damaging impact of global warming. The political aftermath of Rudd's ETS backdown has left the party bruised and tentative. It is tempting for Labor MPs to wish the issue away, that having introduced a carbon tax in 2012, they should now lie low and avoid discussing climate change. This would be a strategic mistake.

In the history of social democracy, there have not been that many issues where science is comprehensively on the side of progressive politics. As an environmental concern, climate change will not go away. It will continue to transform the earth's habitats and, consequently, the way in which we think about economic activity and social organisation.

Labor must lead this debate in Australia. A strategy of withdrawal would cede this political space to the Greens at one extreme and the scaremongering and denialism of the Liberal and National parties at the other. For the remainder of this century and beyond, global warming will be the key transformative issue for left-of-centre politics. Labor has no choice but to think long-term about its consequences and plan for a new model of political economy.

A new discipline
Ross Garnaut once described climate change as a "diabolical policy problem." This is also an appropriate way to think about the challenges facing the Australian Labor movement. Not since the tumultuous post–World War I socialisation debates have the ALP's future direction and purpose been so uncertain. Its organisation is split in two, with the party above suffocating the party below. Its modern identity is also unformed, with the party yet to reconcile competing economic, social and environmental goals. Labor governments have fallen, with heavy swings against them, in New South Wales, Queensland, Victoria and nationally. Those hearty

souls hoping to revive Labor's agenda face a mammoth task – reminiscent of the Yiddish tale of the man sent to wait at the city gates for the millennium. "Big job," he said, "but at least the work is steady."

A task on this scale requires a certain temperament, a positive state of mind. Thus the purpose of this essay is to be constructive, not to rehash in detail things which have gone wrong with the Labor movement. I have provided a summary, and that's sufficient. Bob Carr was right in September 2012 when, in response to the publication of Lindsay Tanner's book *Politics with Purpose,* he said people have grown weary of the endless analysis of Labor's faults.

With a humour typical of his outlook on public life, Carr said the heavy volume of Labor books and essays marked the emergence of a new literary genre, much like vampire novels. My library at home has several shelves of such material: authors highly skilled in identifying problems within the Labor movement but mostly silent on the development of solutions. Tanner's book is no different. It is representative of a modern Labor ailment – a whinging, repetitive obsession with what has gone wrong.

This is somewhat surprising, as Tanner himself has often preached the importance of a constructive approach by the left. He has told the story of walking past an inner-Melbourne building site, reading political posters imploring society to "Stop the Attacks." He wanted to know when the left was going to *start* the attacks – on inequality, on poverty, on environmental decline. This is the mindset Labor needs to adopt: forever positive, forever creative.

Hence there should be a new rigour applied to the writing of books and essays on the ALP: they do not qualify for publication unless they focus on answers – new constructive ideas for the future of social democracy, new positive attacks on entrenched privilege and social injustice. This essay is bound by that discipline, moving beyond the limits of Labor's *Twilight* series.

One last Christmas

I should say something about my motivation in writing this essay. It comes from an obligation to correct a lingering personal failure. Along with Rudd and Julia Gillard, I was a Labor leader drawn from the post-Keating generation of parliamentarians. We were tasked with revitalising the party's agenda after federal Labor's heavy defeat in 1996, but in large part, nearly two decades later, this goal remains unfulfilled.

I had a short period in the job, just fourteen months. Nonetheless, I made no lasting progress in the development of new Labor thinking. Looking back, I came to the leadership too young (at forty-two years of age), with too little life experience (not yet having built a home and raised a family) and with too much of my policy thinking still a work-in-progress. I had done a lot of writing about new ideas for the party, but very little of it was settled in the public arena – that is, tested over time and able to withstand criticism, both from inside the Labor movement and by political opponents.

Rudd and Gillard, in their differing ways, have done better. Rudd delivered an exhilarating election victory in 2007 and, for several years, inspired a generation of true believers to believe again. He is a highly intelligent person with a phenomenal work ethic – the sort of leader who could have successfully addressed Labor's structural challenges. Unhappily, he failed in this task because he put public imagery ahead of the development of public policy.

The legitimacy of Rudd's leadership rested entirely on his standing in the opinion polls. When this dissolved in the first half of 2010, his caucus colleagues, most of whom could not abide the man personally, removed him from the prime ministership. He left office with a newly discovered contempt for Labor's factional system, the so-called faceless men. More tellingly, the key policy issues of his leadership remained unresolved: he failed to develop an effective framework for dealing with climate change, mining taxation and border protection. This was a terrible waste of Rudd's talent – a tragedy made worse by his subsequent role as Labor's parliamentary Destabiliser-in-Chief.

Ultimately, in devoting so much energy to ending Gillard's leadership, Rudd failed to develop a new and appealing agenda for the 2013 election campaign. This was yet another political gift to Tony Abbott and the Coalition. In this respect, Labor in government takes much of the blame for the lack of pressure and scrutiny on its opponents. Having spent three years talking about itself, the party spent just three weeks applying the spotlight to Abbott – a strategic absurdity. Rudd was so consumed by revenge against his internal-party nemesis that he failed to understand his main opponent was the mangy-looking guy in lycra.

While the media cognoscenti have raked over the question of who would have held the highest number of seats – Gillard or Rudd – the real damage to Labor has been below the surface. The ALP is more than a vote-gathering machine, the type of outfit for which journalists forecast finely calibrated electoral results. It is, first and foremost, a political cause, a party with a long history of pushing the envelope on what Australia can be and what Australians can do for each other. The Rudd–Gillard civil war had consequences, not just on the Mackerras pendulum, but for the party's moral core, as a movement worth believing in. Three years of leadership destabilisation, culminating in the late switch to Rudd, left the true believers demoralised.

There have been many criticisms of the ALP's election effort, but the saddest feature was the way in which electorate staff and party members could only bring themselves to campaign half-heartedly. The bastardry of the parliamentary party left them limp and bewildered, a betrayal of the meaning of Labor. Nonetheless, we need to forgive Kevin because, due to his ego and self-absorption, he does not know what he has done. He can only see himself.

Gillard's great skill was on the practical side of government: negotiating successfully with the independents after the 2010 election, navigating a series of legislative reforms through a hung parliament and, for three years, dealing with the disparate sub-factions and fiefdoms of Labor's caucus. Her methodology was that of a transactional leader, a tough-minded doer, rather than a visionary and inspirational figure. Her social policy achievements, especially in fostering bipartisan support for DisabilityCare, are substantial. Ironically, the greatest tribute to her prime ministership came from Abbott and the Liberal Party, when, in the lead-up to September's election, they campaigned as Gillard-lite. Other than on a couple of taxation matters, the Opposition went to the people promising to continue the ALP's legislative and budgetary program.

There was, however, little evidence of Gillard wanting to tackle Labor's structural problems, of pushing forward on party reform. In large part, this was a product of the fraught political environment in which she found herself. History will look back on the debilitating impact of the hung parliament and Rudd's long post-2010 leadership campaign as obstacles to broader change. Fortunately for Gillard, her successor took the pain of a landslide election loss, leaving her, along with Bob Hawke, as the only post-war Labor prime ministers not to lose an election – a landmark achievement. Thus, in the pantheon of party legends, Gillard will always be seen as a dogged fighter, someone who got things done against the odds.

The ALP is at a tipping point in its history. If it does not resolve its underlying contradictions, it might not survive as a viable parliamentary force, shrinking in tandem with its union/working-class base. At the other extreme of possibilities, however, there are opportunities for Labor to fight back from its electoral devastation. Several of the long-term trends in Australian politics are running its way. I have already mentioned the science of global warming – an issue on which, eventually, the right-wing denialists will be routed politically.

Another opportunity for Labor is to be found in the shifting ideological foundations of the conservative parties and their barrackers in the media. In recent years, evidence has emerged of the narrowing base of Australian right-wing politics, relying on a group of activists who practise a fanatical, foreign brand of hard-right dogma, in some respects mimicking the extremism of the Tea Party phenomenon in the United States. After September's election result, it may seem counter-intuitive, but for a range of reasons I believe the people running the Coalition are well removed from the vital middle ground of Australian politics.

Under Tony Abbott's leadership, longstanding political conventions have been trashed as federal politics has become intensely personal and destructive. The reasonable, small-L liberalism of Malcolm Turnbull's leadership is long gone. This is not even John Howard–style conservatism but, rather, an alien political trend in our country – a far-right arrogance and authoritarianism which relentlessly attacks climate scientists, evidence-based policy and anyone in the public debate who cares about social fairness. The democratic traditions of the Liberal Party, tolerating diversity and dissent, have been abandoned in favour of reactionary tactics.

Later in the essay, I look at this development in greater detail and its implications for the two-party contest. The opportunity for Labor, however, is obvious: as the Coalition has moved to a more extreme style of politics, it has distanced itself from the moderate, empirical views of the electoral centre. Labor's period in opposition need not be lengthy. The know-how is available by which the party can deftly reposition itself on economic policy, internal party reform and political strategy. Big swings out can be followed by big swings back in.

Perhaps the ALP can do more than just survive. If it resolves its structural and identity issues – in effect, reinventing itself for the twenty-first century – it has the potential to dominate the new right-wing reactionaries. It can remake itself as a creative centre-left force, meeting the economic aspirations of the new middle class while also addressing underclass poverty – marrying economic growth with social justice. In this way, Labor can win more elections than it loses, reasserting itself as a natural party of government.

I want this essay to assist the next generation of ALP activists in realising that goal, to help them avoid the mistakes of the post-Keating generation. I hope my time out of parliament has allowed my views to mature, to benefit from the process of learning from past errors of election strategy and personal judgment. In my work as a media commentator, I still love an irreverent dig at the system, pushing back against political correctness. But having thought deeply about the challenges facing Labor and watched the old party suffer in recent times, I also have something serious to offer. Whatever my sins, and there have been many, I have been on the right side of the big issues: in the debate about ALP economic policy, on Australia's military involvement in Iraq, in the border-protection/asylum-seeker debate, on the urgency of party reform and on the futility of chopping and changing federal leaders.

I am confident that over time, the recommendations and policy advice in this essay will also hold up well. My contribution comes from a unique perspective: someone with extensive experience inside a political party but with the objectivity one finds in estrangement from the parliamentary system. That is the spirit in which the essay has been written. I have no desire to take a seat at Labor's yuletide dinner table, but perhaps I could drop by one more time, offering some Christmas cheer and constructive advice.

ORGANISATION REFORM

When Bob Hawke, the most popular trade union and political leader in Australian history, declares (as he did in January 2012) that Labor needs to reduce the scale of union influence, one would have thought the debate on party reform had reached a turning point – a stage at which major change had become irresistible. Logic of this kind, however, underestimates the rigidity of the union/factional system. After a brief flurry of media attention, Hawke's comments were blithely ignored by the party's powerbrokers. The system marched on regardless, with the unions continuing to supply the patronage and numbers that fortify factional power.

Hawke put the argument perfectly. "My first love is the trade unions," he said:

> But I would say to [the party] that you need to recognise the facts of life. The party will always be a party which is sympathetic to the interests of working men and women. But that doesn't mean that there has to be what is now an almost suffocating union influence. It will have to change.

He also acknowledged the economic realities confronting the Labor movement:

In one sense, it is sad. But it's a fact of life, there is a fundamental change in the structure of the workforce. Now
there is a much more dispersed workforce, not so easily
organised, not so unionised.

The most direct and effective way of modernising the
ALP would be to end its formal connection to the union
movement, the system of union affiliation. This would reduce
factional power and re-enfranchise the party below. It would
turn Labor into a participatory social democratic party,
unencumbered by direct union/factional influence. But this
is not going to happen. Most obviously, the union chiefs are
not going to sacrifice their power, especially when they have
already lost so much in terms of workforce coverage. To
abandon control of the ALP would be to administer a double
whammy: rendering themselves impotent inside the party, as
well as in the broader economy.

Support for breaking the ALP–union nexus is minimal.
Even a respected party elder like Senator John Faulkner, who
has spoken publicly of the need to weaken the role of "a tiny
coterie of self-interested factional warriors," wants Labor to
maintain its ties to the union movement. A key conclusion of
the 2010 party review Faulkner co-chaired (with Bob Carr
and Steve Bracks) was that "Australia's union movement
remains at the bedrock of the Australian Labor Party …
Maintaining a modern link with the union movement is vital
to Labor's success in the future."

This is a big part of the ALP's emotional framework, the
inability of the true believers to think of a party without

rules and customs binding it to industrial labour. It is argued the union connection keeps Labor in touch with working Australians, even though more than 90 per cent of workers do not belong to unions affiliated to the ALP and, among those that do, only a tiny proportion participate in party forums.

In its final form, this dewy-eyed position is self-defeating. The task of sidelining self-interested factional warriors is made more difficult by the deification of union power – the same force which allows the factions to flourish. Faulkner has criticised a system in which "a Russian doll of nested caucuses sees a tiny minority of MPs exercising a controlling interest over the majority." But in practice, the innermost layer of Labor's Russian doll is a cadre of trade union officials – party bosses with the power to endorse and disendorse ALP members of parliament, especially senators and members of state upper houses.

Larger unions like United Voice, the Australian Manufacturing Workers' Union, the Australian Workers' Union and the Shop Distributive and Allied Employees' Association ("the Shoppies") have purloined groups of MPs they can control, much like Britain's eighteenth-century system of rotten boroughs. If any of these MPs defies a union directive, especially on major issues such as leadership ballots and industrial-relations policy, they risk losing their pre-selection. This coercive power underpins the sub-factional system – the labyrinth of union groupings and personal fiefdoms which, in aggregate, make up the federal and state parliamentary parties. In the decision-making processes of caucus (and also party conferences), the sub-factions combine their numbers into broad left and right factions, usually in the context of extensive horse-trading and compromise.

It is not uncommon for this system to produce perverse outcomes, particularly when MPs and conference delegates are forced into binding votes. As Faulkner has observed:

> Factional binding is inherently undemocratic. It allows a group with 51 per cent of a sub-faction, which then makes up 51 per cent of a faction, which in turn has 51 per cent of the caucus numbers, to force the entire caucus to their position.

With the ALP–union link preserved, reformers need to pursue the next best option. Pragmatically, there is no alternative. The union/faction chiefs will not commit political hara-kiri (by ending union affiliations) but some of them might, in certain circumstances, sponsor significant reforms. Let me explain how this might happen.

Sometimes in politics, organisations which are being eaten away by internal contradiction and under-performance are subject to sweeping change. This occurs when a small but influential band of leaders decides that something dramatic needs to be done to avoid organisational collapse. Vested interests are set aside and the push for modernisation gathers momentum – a program of last-chance reform. High-profile examples of this process include Gough Whitlam's overhaul of the ALP's rules and policy-making in the late 1960s and Tony Blair's creation of New Labour in Britain in the mid-1990s.

The key player for Labor, as ever, is the NSW Right. It is led by two young activists, the outgoing NSW general secretary, Senator Sam Dastyari, and Paul Howes, the head of the AWU. Bruised by the devastation of the Keneally government's 2011 election defeat, they are determined to rebuild the state branch, resurrecting the McKell model of internal party management. This invokes the name and style of William McKell, the NSW premier from 1941 to 1947, who ended the policy adventurism associated with Jack Lang's leadership in the 1930s. McKell was a pragmatic centrist, inspiring the electoral success of the Wran and Carr NSW governments and influencing Keating's approach to economic policy in the 1980s.

Historically, the NSW Right has been strongest when it has embraced the McKell legacy – supporting moderate, incremental Labor reform, fending off the extremism of the party's Socialist Left. This model relies on five principles for running the party:

- The parliamentary party has primacy in the making of policy and legislative decisions.
- The party administration and union movement support the election of Labor governments, without seeking to overturn the policy decisions of the parliamentary party.
- Labor MPs are answerable to the party membership for their pre-selection. State and federal parliamentary parties are answerable to Labor conferences, especially in complying with the rules and principles

of the party platform. When specific policy disputes arise, consultation follows, during which the party leadership offers amendments and concessions to conference and the union movement. Thus the role of the unions is not dogmatic, but transactional – securing a better deal for their members within the framework of parliamentary policy.

- The non-parliamentary party recognises that while it might not agree with every policy outcome, the concessions it receives from Labor governments are always preferable to the policies of Liberal governments.

- In the party's culture, MPs, officials and union leaders are expected to follow high standards of ethical behaviour. As far as possible, Labor should be a meritocracy, most notably in the selection of quality people for safe seats and effective campaigners in marginal seats.

The disintegration of the McKell model over the past decade in New South Wales has been one of the most harmful setbacks in the party's history. This crisis in the NSW Right emerged in four phases, a march of folly in which the proven success of McKell was steadily discarded. By the beginning of 2011, the faction and the party had become ungovernable, with the people of New South Wales consigning state Labor to several terms in opposition.

In each phase, the common thread was trade union arrogance and overreach, by irresponsibly exercising the power of their oligopoly within the state branch. First, the head of the NSW Labor Council, John Robertson, sided with the Socialist Left faction in the development of asylum-seeker policy after the 2001 federal election – a policy weakness from which the party is yet to recover. Second, the NSW unions resolved to undermine Simon Crean's federal leadership in 2002–03 because of his party-reform program (which involved marginally reducing union representation at ALP conferences). Third, Robertson and several right-wing unions refused to support the Iemma government's policy for electricity privatisation in 2007–08, destroying Iemma's leadership and, eventually, the government itself. And finally, at the low point of Sussex Street's ethical decline, union funds within the right-wing Health Services Union were systematically rorted, with police charges laid against a former ALP national president, Michael Williamson, and the federal MP Craig Thomson.

Now Howes and Dastyari are trying to put the faction back together again. They have the advantage of starting with a clean slate: a state parliamentary party routed at the last election and a federal party looking for new leadership and direction. Having studied Labor's recent history, they understand the organisational task before them. In December 2012, for instance, Dastyari declared, "The challenge facing us is, really, reform or die. The Labor Party has to change, it has to reform, it has to be prepared to embrace big ideas."

It is a long time since a senior NSW Right figure has spoken this way. Howes and Dastyari know what needs to be done to improve the party's prospects, both in terms of organisational change and policy development. They are two important voices for modernisation at a national level, for rebuilding the McKell model in New South Wales and then applying its benefits to federal Labor. Anyone who wants the party to prosper will want these young enthusiasts to turn their words into action, to seize a once-in-a-generation opportunity for change.

Dastyari's big idea is the introduction of primaries for the selection of Labor candidates. This was trialled in the City of Sydney mayoral election in 2012, with branch members allotted half of the pre-selection votes and the local community the other half. It resulted in the participation of 341 party members and 3612 community voters (or 5.1 per cent of the general electorate) – an encouraging result, albeit in an inner-city area with a relatively strong culture of political involvement. The NSW party now plans to conduct primary ballots for the selection of candidates in five winnable seats for the 2015 state election.

So far, the internal party debate about pre-selections has focused on two issues: their capacity to attract new branch members and their usefulness in winning marginal seats. While these are not insignificant matters, there is something more important to consider. Primary pre-selections have the potential to transform the party's culture by reconnecting it to one of the key drivers of Labor achievement: the community engagement which can produce outstanding party leaders and policies. For this reason alone, the primary system should be supported.

Last-chance reform

One of the catchcries of the thoroughbred breeding industry, in which I take a keen interest, is "You only need one" – meaning that one good galloper can set up a breeder for life, increasing the value of young horses related to the star performer. The Labor Party is no different. Its most successful periods of reform are characterised by one inspiring leader, one creative spark for policy-making success. Invariably, the spark has come from the leader's personal experience, from perspectives and ideas gleaned from grassroots political participation.

The party's four great reformers, John Curtin, Ben Chifley, Gough Whitlam and Paul Keating, each followed this pattern: the young Curtin crusading for social justice with the Salvation Army on the working-class streets of Brunswick, Melbourne; Chifley, first and foremost a son of Bathurst in central NSW, a servant of the local community, not just as a federal MP, treasurer and prime minister but also as an Abercrombie Shire councillor; Whitlam, raising a young family in Cabramatta in Sydney's south-west, gathering ideas for education, health and urban policy from his electorate; and finally, the attentive young Keating, bruised by his father's frustration in trying to raise bank finance for the family's small manufacturing business – a personal catalyst for the deregulation of Australia's financial system in the 1980s.

You only need one. One quality leader to emerge with a bundle of policies and know-how derived from hands-on experience in the electorate. This is, from the time of its founding, how the ALP is supposed to function – giving working people from the grassroots of politics a voice in the legislative process. The ideal was for mass participation: every working person a unionist, every unionist a branch member.

While in the modern era the ideal is no longer attainable, the policy leadership process can be. No one expects large numbers of people to join parties anymore – apathy and busy lifestyles have ended this possibility. At a local level, the remaining political energy for Labor now revolves around ambition: young people and established activists getting involved, hoping to progress through the party and become members of parliament. Labor needs to harness this personal drive and activity, using it as a way of forcing pre-selection hopefuls to embed themselves in community politics.

The pathway to parliament should not be through union/factional patronage. It should be based on the Curtin/Chifley/Whitlam/Keating precedent: a capacity to work with local organisations, learning lessons about the public's needs and converting this experience into Labor policy. Primary pre-selections are the best mechanism for re-establishing this culture. They ensure that nobody can become a Labor candidate without forging a reputation for community engagement, and winning the trust of branch members, community groups and progressively minded residents.

The party below has lost a lot over the past thirty years. All it has left is the ambition of new people joining. Unless it makes good use of this motivation, Labor's membership crisis will continue to worsen. Primary pre-selections can heal the party's organisational split: the party above ceding power to branch members and community voters in the selection of parliamentary candidates. This would shift Labor's centre of gravity, taking the arrogance out of the factional system and emphasising the importance of community-based policy development.

Centralised candidate selection by state executives and the national executive would end, including for upper-house members. There is no reason why senators and state members of legislative councils could not be chosen through 50/50 primaries, cleaning out the sub-factional rotten boroughs. As the union/factional system has intensified, the quality of ALP upper-house members has deteriorated. The first priority for these MPs is factional organisation, ignoring the importance of policy work. Their contact with the electorate tends to be desultory, weakening the party's community credentials. With upper-house candidates subject to state-wide primaries, it would be possible for state branches to ballot for lower-house seats on the same day – a Super-Saturday effect.

In establishing this system, I would add an extra stage to the primaries process: the vetting of candidates to encourage genuine community involvement. One of the dangers of primaries is poorly motivated candidates who circumvent the system. An obvious risk is the targeting of ethnic groups with enticements and sweetheart deals – a backdoor form of ethnic branch-stacking. Excessive campaign expenditure could be another problem, as per the US experience.

Thus the primaries should operate according to the following structure and timetable:

- Nine months before the scheduled primary, the party calls for expressions of interest for a particular seat.
- Those who nominate go through an assessment process by a panel comprising party elders (members respected across factional lines, such as Faulkner and Iemma), local branch office-bearers, a Labor Council representative and a state branch official.
- In determining eligibility to contest the primary, the panel applies certain criteria (a track record of local community engagement, public-speaking ability and policy-making credentials) and sets certain tasks (such as organising public meetings on local issues and presenting policy papers to Labor think-tanks). The objective is to maximise the party's community presence and gauge the ability of candidates not only to win their seats, but also to serve as parliamentary frontbenchers.
- The vetted candidates are announced two months before the primary ballot, giving them ample time to run for the position (within strict campaign-expenditure limits).

There are other things Labor can do to improve its participatory credentials. Many of these ideas are set out in the Faulkner/Bracks/Carr report – such as allowing like-minded organisations (not just trade unions) to affiliate to the party, directly electing national conference delegates and state branch presidents, and adopting a community-organising model for local branches. While helpful in opening up party forums, these are not culture-changing proposals. The point of last-chance reform is to recognise how the long-term decline of an organisation can only be fixed by transforming its structure and ethos. Given the impossibility of breaking the union nexus, Labor's best hope is the introduction of primary pre-selections.

The Rudd effect

Out of the crisis of the three-year Rudd–Gillard leadership struggle, a significant change has been made to the way in which the federal parliamentary Labor Party elects its leader. A weighted franchise allocating 50 per cent voting power to MPs and 50 per cent to rank-and-file members has been introduced. For the first time, the party membership will have a direct say in the affairs of the federal caucus – choosing between Anthony Albanese and Bill Shorten for Labor's leadership in opposition.

This is the most important legacy of Rudd's truncated second prime-ministerial term. He instigated the change for two strategic reasons: to dilute the power of the sub-factional chiefs who moved against him in June 2010; and to restore stability to the tenure of federal leaders. Since 2001, Labor has had seven leadership changes – a revolving door which turns, on average, every twenty months. Chaos of this kind has undermined public confidence in the capacity of ALP leaders to do the job, building an impression they are permanently on probation at the whim of so-called faceless men.

Motivated by revenge, Rudd has been Labor's accidental reformer. Nonetheless, whether by accident or altruism, rule changes to give party members a say in the election of the parliamentary leader are welcome. The outgoing leader has placed the spotlight on the role of the sub-factional chiefs who dominate caucus, the opportunistic powerbrokers who have spun the revolving door on a regular basis. They are the clearest, most prominent sign of what factional machine politics has done to the cause of Labor. It is worthwhile, therefore, to review the history of the sub-factional system and propose rule changes to put these political warlords out of business.

My 2005 diaries provided the first detailed account of this problem. It explained the changing nature of the factional system: how the large, relatively stable left- and right-wing blocs of the 1980s had dissolved into a series of bickering sub-factions. The ALP was no longer a cohesive party, but a loose federation of feudal-style warlords, each practising the politics of self-interested manipulation and treachery.

These smaller groupings, while based on personality and geographic factors, were also underpinned by union control. The Victorian Right, for instance, had broken into a Crean group, a Conroy group and the Shoppies. My book listed eighteen sub-factions, with an average membership of just five MPs.

Why did the Labor caucus fragment so badly? In the 1990s, three factors combined to reshape the party's structure. The first was the Australian Council of Trade Unions' program of union amalgamations, moving from craft-based representation to an industry-based system. These super-unions had the numerical strength at state Labor conferences to demand upper-house spots, while also cutting deals to have union officials pre-selected for lower-house seats. From around the country, a steady flow of union representatives entered federal parliament, forming sub-factional cliques.

Another significant change in Australia's industrial base also sharpened the union focus on federal politics. The Greiner revolution in New South Wales and Kennett reforms in Victoria corporatised and privatised state government utilities. Previously, Labor-affiliated trade unions had been closely involved in state issues, using their influence inside the party to protect the job security of members employed by state service providers. Once this leverage was lost, the union bosses took a bigger interest in national politics as a way of exercising their authority, a process accelerated by the transfer of state government industrial relations powers to the Commonwealth. By the time of the 2007 WorkChoices election, the union/sub-factional nexus in Canberra had been sealed.

The third factor arose from the culture of factionalism itself. In the 1980s and '90s, as grassroots activism declined and the party more closely resembled an oligarchy, positions of power were viewed as more important than policy positions. Every two-bit apparatchik wanted to be the next Graham Richardson or Robert Ray. These would-be warlords developed power bases inside Labor's state branches, inevitably securing parliamentary seats for themselves. Whereas a state branch might have had three or four groups clustered around the new powerbrokers (a manageable number), when multiplied nationally, it produced eighteen to twenty-four sub-factions jostling for control in federal caucus – a formula for anarchy.

Like an archaeologist digging through the sediment of election results, one can identify each wave of machine men entering federal parliament. In 1993, three former state secretaries won seats: Wayne Swan in Queensland and Stephen Smith and Chris Evans in Western Australia. From different parts of the Victorian Left, Kim Carr and Alan Griffin joined the caucus.

Carr took John Button's spot in the Senate, a hard-line machine man replacing a factionally non-aligned, irreverent spirit in the party. Senator Carr's parliamentary career is a case study in how sub-factional and union patronage shapes the development of ALP economic policy. In successive leadership ballots, Carr supported Simon Crean against Kim Beazley in 2003, Rudd against Beazley in 2006 and Rudd against Gillard in 2013 – in each case, backing candidates who promised to make him the party's spokesperson on industry policy. Why did this matter to him? Carr's sub-factional base relies heavily on the support of the AMWU, hence his decision as industry minister to pay large public subsidies to industries in which the AMWU has members, most notably car manufacturing. Public money was used to prop up Carr's sub-factional patron.

In 1996, Albanese and Martin Ferguson were elected to parliament, their distrust and dislike of each other splitting the national Left faction into "hard" (Albanese) and "soft" (Ferguson) groupings. From Victoria, Stephen Conroy filled Gareth Evans' upper-house vacancy – another sign of how policy wonks in the Senate were being replaced by union-aligned numbers men. Throughout Labor's time in opposition, each of the super-unions significantly increased its federal representation.

And so the little Richos continued to emerge: in 2004, Tony Burke and Chris Bowen from the NSW Right. In 2007, a major intake: Shorten, Richard Marles, Mark Butler, Don Farrell, Mark Arbib, David Feeney and Doug Cameron. In the 2010–13 caucus of 102 members, Labor had twenty-four sub-factional chiefs. After the recent election, the concentration of machine men in caucus is even greater, given their strength in holding down Senate spots and safe House of Representatives seats. Of the seventeen MPs and candidates who lost Labor-held lower house seats on 7 September 2013, none of them were sub-factional leaders.

One does not need to be a game-theory expert to appreciate the instability of this system. It encourages opportunists to switch from one sub-faction to another, with a single vote changing the internal balance of power. It also legitimises the role of powerbrokers, emboldening them to advance their group's interests ahead of the party's interests. To maintain the support of their followers, these MPs need to appear influential, immersing themselves in caucus manoeuvring and back-stabbing. Over the past twelve years, in exercising their power to determine the parliamentary leader, the sub-factional chiefs have fallen into one of two categories: either supporting the incumbent (on the basis that he or she shows them sufficient respect and deference) or destabilising in favour of someone more compliant.

This is why the party has experienced constant leadership turmoil. If, by some miracle, the caucus united behind its leader, the warlords would manufacture other areas of dispute – a system of institutionalised instability. They only survive by notching up power-play victories, by leaking and conniving, trying to convince their followers they are the cleverest operator in the room. For their subordinates, it's the omnipresent fear of knowing if they betray or even disobey their boss, he can destroy them politically. Thus sub-factional warlords rely on public notoriety to cultivate deference from their followers – explaining, in part, their closeness to the press gallery.

The sub-factional culture of self-important meddling has infected the entire caucus. Backbench MPs are in the habit of passing daily judgment on the performance of the leader, much like Olympic diving judges holding up scorecards. Seat-fillers who have spent decades in parliament without any prospect of frontbench promotion see themselves as experts on how to run the show. Even first-term backbenchers like Ed Husic, Laura Smyth and Stephen Jones took it upon themselves to white-ant Gillard's leadership – an extraordinary display of arrogance.

While the media saw Labor's leadership contest through the prism of Rudd's and Gillard's personalities, its driving force internally was sub-factional ambition to be on the winning side. If machine men like Carr, Albanese, Shorten and Simon Crean had not entertained Rudd's ambitions, the government would not have imploded. Tanya Plibersek was right on election night when she said, "I'd give us nine out of ten for governing the country; I'd give us zero out of ten for governing ourselves." Labor's defeated candidate in Forde, Peter Beattie, has said, "The election was winnable but the public had had enough of the in-fighting." Gillard and Rudd didn't kill the government, the sub-factions did.

Breaking sub-factional power

With the wrong instincts and motivations, the warlords are a malevolent influence on Labor. Carr's approach to industry policy is typical of how they approach public policy, putting sectional interests ahead of national economic needs. In their exercise of authority inside the party, the sub-factional chiefs are anti-egalitarian. Their methods are the antithesis of Labor's ideals for social fairness, of the plain, earthy values we associate with Chifley's "Light on the Hill."

Take, for instance, a telling passage in Richardson's memoirs, *Whatever It Takes*. In a moment of candour, looking back on his early years as a right-wing organiser, he wrote:

> Meeting the right people in the Labor Party was not part of a brilliant strategy, [rather] I wanted to meet them because everything they did fascinated me ... And while most people who attain positions of power may be reluctant to say so in these terms, the prospect of people deferring to me one day – in the way they were deferring to the "right people" I was beginning to meet – was pretty attractive.

This is not how policy-oriented people look at politics. They see a public problem and try to apply a public policy solution – on our side, the quest for social justice. But for Richardson and his successors, the party machine offers special rewards, in the form of careerism and social status. Sub-factional powerbrokers do not look at their colleagues as equals, but as underlings who need to defer to them. Thus they practise the politics of intimidation, standing over party members. This has created feudal pecking orders inside the Labor movement, against the grain of how an egalitarian organisation should function.

The rot in Labor's culture started when Richardson's view of politics became the prevailing view among the party's apparatchiks. The sub-factional ethos of status and manipulation is a stain on Labor's spirit, affecting its work at all levels. Unless it is excised, more scandals like the HSU affair and the corruption of Labor ministers Eddie Obeid and Ian Macdonald in New South Wales are inevitable. It is not possible to create a self-serving culture inside the party without these values spilling over into the misuse of union and government resources. If Labor tolerates a self-interested system internally, it should not be surprised that self-interested individuals, operating in the name of the ALP, end up behaving corruptly.

Political insiders often ask how someone like Richardson from the right faction and Albanese from the left can be friends. The answer is obvious: they exercise sub-factional power in complementary ways. Richardson recruited Obeid to the NSW parliament, while Albanese granted Macdonald an extra term in the Legislative Council, during which the abuse of mining leases occurred. For Labor, no long-term good ever comes from factional wheeling and dealing.

The notion that an inner-city warlord like Albanese is now the true spirit of Labor reveals how badly the party has deteriorated. Instead of testing someone's quality by asking how well they work the numbers or how assiduously they cultivate the media, Labor needs to return to a basic understanding of political virtue: is someone right or wrong on major issues? In Albanese's case, he was wrong on boat-people policy, he has been wrong on economic policy for twenty years, he was wrong in his undermining of Gillard and restoration of Rudd and, most damaging of all, he was wrong to prop up Macdonald. In September's election campaign, he was wrong to associate with Craig Thomson. This is not the sort of person on whom the Labor movement can build a viable future. The party needs an extended period of focusing on right and wrong, instead of the self-serving bravado of machine politics.

In their power and reach, the sub-factions effectively own the party. Unless this problem is dealt with, Labor's future will continue to shrivel. Each of the party's structural problems – its organisational malaise, its identity crisis, its missed opportunities on economic policy, its leadership instability and its exposure to corruption scandals – comes from the union-sponsored sub-factional network. It is at the epicentre of what's gone wrong. Just as it's impossible to run other organisations, public and private sector, with every fourth person trying to control outcomes for everyone else, federal Labor has become anarchical.

The core purpose of organisational reform must be to break the warlords' franchise. Unfortunately, Rudd's reform package fails to fully achieve this goal. It is based on an unsatisfactory compromise: taking away 50 per cent of the power of the sub-factions to elect the federal leader, but restoring 100 per cent of their power to pick Labor's frontbench. After his 2007 election victory, Rudd himself selected the new ministry.

This is why machine men like Albanese and Carr have supported Rudd's 2013 proposals: in terms of manipulating caucus outcomes, they are 50 per cent in front. One of the prerogatives they truly treasure – claiming frontbench spots for their small band of caucus followers – is back in their hands. Anyone wanting to understand the chaos of this system from the last time it was used (after the 2004 election) should read *The Latham Diaries* (pages 361–8).

In advocating organisational change, I do not expect Labor to re-emerge as a party of mass membership. Rather, the rationale for reform is to improve the behavioural and incentives system inside the party, neutering the corrosive sub-factional influence. Ultimately, the only solution to problems caused by the concentration of political power is a program of devolution. Rule changes are needed on four fronts:

- In the election of the parliamentary leader, giving rank-and-file members 100 per cent of the voting franchise.
- Allowing the leader to select the frontbench, free from sub-factional pressures.
- Reducing trade union representation at party conferences to match union coverage in the workforce

(down from the current 50 per cent franchise to no more than 20 per cent).

- Using community pre-selections to choose Labor's election candidates, ending the system of sub-factional deal-making.

In opposition, nothing will change unless the party changes its rules and culture. The names and personalities no longer matter. The party has made itself ungovernable and unless solutions are found, the public will not allow it to govern the nation. If Rudd's return is to have any lasting benefit, it must be to extend his tentative attempt at reform into a comprehensive program of ALP democratisation.

Perhaps Tony Abbott's government will be hopeless and fall over. But if it's halfway competent, it will enjoy a long period in power simply because of the dysfunctionality of its opponents. This is what is so frustrating about Labor's decline. The know-how exists to heal the party: to devolve power at all levels, to pre-select MPs unbeholden to union bosses, to end the warlords' control of caucus. It simply requires reformist leadership and political common sense to make it happen.

A POST-LEFT ELECTORATE

The authentic Labor tradition is not one of grand theories and dogma. It is a tradition of community engagement – the legacy of Curtin, Chifley, Whitlam, Keating and, at state level, McKell. This is an empirical style of policy development, responding to the needs of people who look to Labor for better opportunities in life. If any of these leaders represented a country town or outer-suburban constituency today, what would they find?

Compared to their period in parliament, they would notice an all-encompassing change. That is, the disintegration of the traditional institutions of the left: organised labour, working-class solidarity and mass meetings of a political nature. There is no longer any central mechanism for bringing together progressively-minded people in local electorates. If Labor is to have a future, it must be a post-left future. It can no longer rely on the politics of mass scale and common membership.

Electoral opinions and interests are now highly dispersed, spread across individuals, diverse family types and small-scale community groups. Majority beliefs still exist, of course, but in a notional way, without the organisational rallying points of the past. Few community bodies can claim to speak on behalf of a significant proportion of citizens. With higher levels of education and better access to information, people are more likely to make up their own minds on issues, bypassing the views of interest groups and media commentators.

The most pervasive public belief is economic aspiration. The sons and daughters of the working class have had a taste of financial success and they want more. In this task, they do not expect governments to control economic outcomes, but rather to foster an environment in which individuals, through hard work and enterprise, can advance themselves. Flexible and effective service delivery is all-important, as people juggle the demands of work, education and family.

These values are underpinned by an earthy, no-nonsense approach to politics. If the two-party system appears negative and overly adversarial, people lose interest and disengage. If parents see teachers struggling to achieve results in their local public school, they promptly switch to the non-government sector. The most significant aspiration of all is for the education of the next generation.

If taxpayers see evidence of welfare recipients taking advantage of the system, they want governments to take a tougher approach. If local residents experience problems with ethnic crime gangs, they become sceptical about the composition of Australia's migration program. On the big sweeping claims of public life, such as the impact of climate change, people want hard evidence: expert information which corresponds with their own experience. Big ideas are still possible in politics, but first they must prove their credibility and relevance on a smaller scale.

A similar type of empiricism is applied to social values. Some of the staples of conservative politics are in decline. After several generations of marriage failure and patched-up family arrangements, society is far more tolerant of diversity in the home. The traditional nuclear family model, with its white picket fence imagery, is no longer the only acceptable family structure. Gay relationships, unmarried couples and shared parenting (in which children from broken relationships move between one home and another) have a legitimacy which was unthinkable thirty years ago.

Labor needs to be a conduit for these majority values. As a party of electoral politics, it has no choice but to move with the electoral tide. Despite the wishes of many on the left, it is not possible to vote in a new electorate. The challenge for Labor is to shape, through community engagement, public opinion for egalitarian purposes. In some areas, such as family values, social trends are moving in its favour. In other fields, most notably economic aspiration, the party needs to rethink its policies and the way it communicates them to the electorate.

This is a forgotten aspect of the Whitlam/Keating leadership model: the power of persuasion. Whitlam spent his years in opposition arguing and re-arguing the case for reform, such as universal health insurance and needs-based schools funding. Similarly, Keating saw himself not just as an economic reformer but also as a public educator, explaining the workings and advantages of open-market economics. Contrast this approach, for instance, with the Gillard government's precipitate introduction of a carbon tax and the political problems which followed.

This is where Labor's culture needs to change. Inside the party, factional powerbrokers have grown accustomed to telling people what to do. When applied outside the party, this technique is inadequate – setting back the reform cause with its overtones of arrogance and deceit. The skills of argument and public persuasion have been lost. Among the many union officials who have become Labor senators, some can barely string two sentences together. This is another compelling reason for the introduction of community pre-selections: ensuring the party's best debaters and persuaders can win seats in parliament.

Accepting the Keating Settlement

Among the mistakes of modern Labor, none has been more frustrating than its failure to capitalise on the Keating economic legacy. In the history of the Labor movement, one can readily draw up a long list of policy failures. White Australia, industry protection, population decentralisation, broadacre public-housing estates, indigenous-welfare policy and Rudd's education revolution come to mind. It is far harder to identify enduring achievements – policies which were so correct, so successful that not even Coalition governments dismantled them. Here one thinks of Medicare, engagement with China and some of the Hawke government's education initiatives (such as lifting school retention rates).

This is what makes Labor's ambivalence about Keating's program so bizarre. Among the achievements of ALP governments since federation, the 1983–96 reforms stand out: creating the policy settings for twenty years of low inflationary growth and unprecedented wealth creation. For the first time, suburban workers grabbed a significant slice of Australia's economic expansion. They were able to move into better jobs or obtain capital funding and start their own enterprises. The National Centre for Social and Economic Modelling (NATSEM) has calculated that since 1984, real disposable incomes in Australia have increased by 20 per cent – leaving the average family $224 per week better off in real terms.

Importantly, this rising tide has lifted all boats, as measured by income. As the 2012 NATSEM report concluded:

> A particularly surprising result is that, in terms of percentage gain over the cost of living, we find the lowest income households have actually managed a small claw back compared to the highest income group. Quintile one income growth [the lowest 20 per cent band] exceeded the cost of living over the past 27 years by 27 per cent, while the top income quintile outpaced [living costs] by only 19 per cent.

Given that welfare recipients experienced an 11.9 per cent increase, the result for wage-earners in the bottom income quintile was very strong. In the other income bands, there is further evidence of the equalising impact of Keating's reforms. The second quintile (20–40 per cent of income levels) experienced a large gain in real disposable income (30.5 per cent), while quintiles three (19.5) and four (14.6) also improved but by smaller amounts.

TABLE 1. Income gains after living-cost changes

	1984 TO 2009–10		2003–04 TO 2009–10	
	$ PW**	% GAIN*	$ PW	% GAIN
INCOME QUINTILE				
Q1 (LOW)	$93	27.1%	$42	10.7%
Q2	$191	30.5%	$105	14.7%
Q3	$200	19.5%	$153	14.2%
Q4	$211	14.6%	$250	17.8%
Q5 (HIGH)	$429	19.1%	$576	27.4%
SOURCE OF INCOME				
Wages and salaries	$170	11.3%	$228	15.9%
Business	$175	15.6%	$208	19.1%
Government benefits	$61	11.9%	$69	13.7%
Other	$547	64.8%	$426	44.1%
FAMILY TYPE				
Couple and children	$475	34.0%	$328	21.2%
Single parents	$257	37.4%	$59	6.6%
Couple only	$181	16.0%	$220	20.0%
Lone person	$86	14.0%	$115	19.8%
Other family/group	-$74	-4.0%	$266	17.4%
TENURE TYPE				
Outright owner	$241	27.0%	$228	25.2%
Purchaser	$254	16.8%	$254	16.9%
Renter	$112	10.7%	$173	17.5%
Other	$199	23.9%	$197	23.7%
WORKING FAMILIES	$306	22.1%	$238	16.4%
ALL	$199	19.9%	$224	19.9%

* Equivalised income.
** Actual income.
Source: ABS and NATSEM.

For all the commentary about "Howard's battlers" and Rudd's "working families under financial pressure," the statistical evidence suggests a different dynamic. When it came to raising living standards for the lowest paid, Keating's role was paramount, overshadowing the contribution of his two prime-ministerial successors.

This is what Laborism is supposed to achieve: to lift up the bottom, to break down class barriers and to make social mobility possible. Not surprisingly, this process has ignited further aspiration, even greater ambition for the economic success of the next generation. What was the old working class supposed to do, having enjoyed more money in its kick? Go back to low-paid factory work and rented fibro cottages? The practical argument against Keating's achievements is nonsensical. How can any of Labor's true believers campaign against such a stunning record of success?

Yet this is what large sections of the Labor movement have been doing. When Keating retired from parliament, having set up Australia's miracle economy, he was sceptical about the durability of free-market economics inside the party. "I got all those changes through," he told me in his retirement years, "but our people never really believed it, they never really believed in markets and competition."

He was right. One of the first decisions of Kim Beazley and Simon Crean in opposition was to distance themselves from Keating economics. "Labor Buries Keating," the *Business Review Weekly* screeched in March 1997, as Crean heralded a return to industry planning and subsidisation. This was an electoral gift to the Howard government, in its declaration that the ALP no longer saw itself as responsible for national economic outcomes and reform. A legacy once so abandoned is doubly difficult to retrieve.

The record of the Rudd and Gillard governments were no better. After 2007, two major statements of economic ideology were issued, both in the *Monthly*, both deviating from the Keating ethos of competition and deregulation. In February 2009, Rudd declared:

> the great neoliberal experiment of the past thirty years has failed … the emperor has no clothes. Neoliberalism, and the free-market fundamentalism it has produced, has been revealed as little more than personal greed dressed up as an economic philosophy.

The NATSEM figures render such a claim ridiculous. Far from walking the streets naked, Australia's neoliberal reforms have been a sartorial success. Due to reductions in tariffs, average prices for footwear and clothing in Australia have fallen since 1984 – making them more affordable for emperors and citizens alike.

With the passing of time, it is too easily forgotten how pompously wrong Rudd was in his analysis of the global financial crisis. Much like a Hegelian theorist, he opined in the opening of his essay:

> From time to time in human history there occur events of a truly seismic significance, events that mark a turning point between one epoch and the next, when one

orthodoxy is overthrown and another takes its place. The significance of these events is rarely apparent as they unfold: it becomes clear only in retrospect, when observed from the commanding heights of history.

Five years later, history's verdict is still clear: open, free markets work better than any leftist alternative.

The second essay, by Treasurer Wayne Swan in March 2012, launched a populist critique of market economics and its leading beneficiaries – in particular, the Australian mining billionaires Clive Palmer, Andrew Forrest and Gina Rinehart. Swan's polemic was the perfect expression of an age-old Labor dilemma: how to regulate and restrict capitalists without harming the economic prospects of the workers they employ.

In his day job, the treasurer was responsible for making mining and other companies more profitable. It's what we call the national economic interest. Yet as a Labor partisan, never truly comfortable with a system of profit-based capitalism, Swan wanted to damage Palmer, Forrest and Rinehart. The two goals, of course, were incompatible. Whether we like it or not, what's good for capital investment in the economy is also good for employment levels, wages and working conditions.

The ALP has been grappling with this contradiction for more than a century. One of the powerful themes of early twentieth-century Laborism was "the Money Power" – a fierce condemnation of financiers as the root cause of social evil. Thus the one industry Labor tried to nationalise was the banking system, through the Chifley government's failed bank nationalisation legislation in 1947. Even during the term of the Whitlam government, which seemed modern in many respects, anti-capitalism was prevalent, especially in treasurer Jim Cairns's rhetoric and Rex Connor's attitude to the energy and mining sectors.

The first senior Labor politician to resolve this tension was Keating. He accepted the inevitability of profit-based economics, dispensing with Labor's long-running delusion that the system could be planned, regulated or manipulated for other purposes. The genius of Keating's approach was to take the underlying rationale of capitalism – open-market competition – and use it for two strategic, left-of-centre goals.

The first was to make life uncomfortable for monopoly and oligopoly capitalists. As a young MP, Keating had witnessed the contradictions of Australian industry policy. Markets are supposed to foster a competitive struggle among suppliers. Yet in the 1960s, under the Country Party leader John McEwen, selected industries were afforded tariff protection and sub-sidisation. Large parts of the Labor movement supported this policy, an accommodation between the captains of industry and trade unionism.

Companies were shielded from competition, at an ongoing cost to Australian consumers and taxpayers. Short-term profit-ability was maintained, not through the competitive necessity of upgrading technology, work practices, corporate manage-ment and productivity, but by living off subsidies and tariff walls. Politically, Keating saw this as a mug's game, in which Labor helped capitalists live a slothful, non-competitive exis-tence, yet at election time these same companies endorsed and funded the Coalition. Economically, protectionism ran down plant investments and workforce skills, condemning Australian labour to the misery of low-paid, repetitive work.

Keating's second objective was to use competition policy as a stimulus for economic growth, creating room for productivity-linked wage increases. Through financial deregulation and compulsory superannuation, workers also enjoyed improved access to capital, sparking a new generation of entrepreneurialism. As the NATSEM figures show, the strategy ratcheted up living standards, allowing low-income earners to progress at a faster rate than high-income earners. This was a wonderfully creative piece of cross-over politics: using a right-wing rationale (free-market competition) to achieve the traditional Labor goals of equity and prosperity.

In effect, in the Australian economy, it replaced McEwenite preferment with the Keating Settlement. The proven success of the model has simplified the task of economic policy-making. There is now just one question for Labor parliamentarians to ask: what would Keating do? Support for the Keating Settlement should be as automatic as the party's endorsement of Medicare or its belief in looking after the frail aged and disabled.

Any other approach, any ongoing debate about economic principles, is a waste of the party's time and resources. Electorally, it also sends a confusing message, dulling the faith of aspirational voters in the party's values and competence. For social democrats, there are so few policy issues in which the contest of ideas has been settled, in which the evidence is so compelling that they can move on to other, unresolved questions. This is the tragedy of modern Labor: the debate about the Keating Settlement is far from settled.

The problem, as in so many areas, is rent-seeking trade unionism. For rotten-borough senators like Kim Carr and Doug Cameron, representing the AMWU, the big economic question is: what does my union want me to do? Their sole interest is in propping up declining manufacturing businesses and employment. Their only answer is a throwback to McEwenism: preferment, protectionism and subsidisation.

The worst example of this process is the federal government's continued financial support for car manufacturing – subsidies which, for thirty-five years, have failed to make the industry internationally competitive and to prevent ongoing redundancies. The spread of globalisation has only made McEwenism a bigger mug's game. With the increased mobility of capital, public subsidies offer only temporary relief. They encourage companies and unions to plead for even larger hand-outs, forever threatening governments with the relocation of investment offshore. In practice, industry welfare stifles innovation and plant modernisation – a competitive disadvantage. Beyond its immediate impact, government financial support is a job destroyer, not a job saver.

The Keating Settlement is not only an economic growth and distribution strategy. It is also an economic-restructuring policy, lifting the Australian workforce into high-skill, high-wage employment. An important part of the adjustment process is to assist blue-collar workers made redundant by the decline of smokestack manufacturing. Through retraining and labour market programs they can find better jobs elsewhere, especially in an economy near full employment.

In practical terms, only a small proportion of Australians lament the decline of old manufacturing jobs. The nation's parents have no desire for their children to work in the same jobs their grandparents once held: dirty, repetitive, low-paid production-line employment. Their aspiration, not surprisingly, is for the clean, creative professional jobs of the new economy. Hence the emphasis on education – conferring the expertise that secures a lifetime of high earnings. Economically and politically, industry welfare is a dead-end debate for Labor.

Instead of artificially supporting basket-case capital, the trade union movement should accept the inevitability of restructuring and retraining. It should end Labor's long-running agony over economic policy and accept the Keating Settlement. This is the only way in which the party can keep faith with the aspirational class it created in the 1980s and '90s, presenting itself as pro-growth, pro-skills and pro-economic modernisation. If there is one thing worse than Labor forfeiting the Keating legacy, it is the prospect of never reclaiming it.

With the party's heavy 2013 election loss, the urgency in rethinking its stance on economic policy has become even sharper. Just as Bill Hayden as Opposition leader in the late 1970s worked overtime in rebuilding Labor's budgetary credentials after the profligacy of the Whitlam years, the new Opposition leadership needs to rebuild its reputation for fiscal responsibility. It also has to undo the damage caused by Rudd's recklessness on industry policy.

Despite promising "a new way," the resurrected leader campaigned as an old-fashioned Queensland state development advocate, reviving discredited themes such as government-led northern development and Hansonite concerns about foreign investment. This was the real Rudd, a long-time believer in industry subsidies, government intervention and Keynesian pump-priming. His 2007 claim to being an "economic conservative" had been an aberration, a campaign convenience designed to defeat John Howard, but never to be acted on in government.

Most disconcerting of all, in the second-last week of the campaign, at a rally in Melbourne's shipyards accompanied by industry minister Kim Carr, the outgoing prime minister declared, "I am, in my heart of hearts, an Australian economic nationalist," who saw his primary mission as "protecting manufacturing jobs." No Labor leader had spoken this way since Arthur Calwell in the 1960s. Rudd's new way was actually a throwback to the worst instincts of ALP isolationism.

It is hard to describe the tragedy of what Rudd has done. After two decades of unbroken economic growth and prosperity generated by the Keating model, the greatest policy success story in Labor history, Rudd campaigned in direct contradiction of these economic principles. He trashed the party's record and hastened his own exit from high office. It was, without question, the low point in Labor's six years in government.

It need not be this way. The know-how, experience and economic legacy exists by which Labor can reclaim the Keating model. It comes down to a question of belief and electoral relevance. The journey back against a large Coalition majority in the House of Representatives does not lie in the clap-trap of anti-market, anti-competitive policies. After the party's heavy defeat in 1996, Beazley and Crean tried this approach, but all it did was extend our time in opposition. We would have won the 1998 election if swinging middle-class voters believed in Labor's economic credentials. The only proven way by which the party can appeal to the nation's rising aspirational class is to embrace the policy ethos which transformed Australia in the first place.

Public persuasion

When Labor walked away from the Keating Settlement, it lost more than economic credibility. It also lost a key part of the Keating schema: the capacity to educate the public about the transformative impact of open-market economics on other aspects of national life. In elected office, where there is no belief, there can be no persuasion. This was a striking feature of Labor's six years in government – the reluctance of senior ministers to talk about the economy beyond the daily release of financial data. They failed to make the case for ongoing structural change and for a new way of thinking about the relationship between politics and economics.

The last major reform of the Keating government was the introduction of National Competition Policy in 1995, applying commercial principles to the utility, transport and telecommunications functions of the public sector. Federal and state authorities were corporatised, creating a level playing field for them and their privately owned competitors. Real-cost pricing and efficient staffing levels were introduced across most jurisdictions. Thus the executive wing of government lost its capacity to directly control the pricing decisions of these instrumentalities. In large part, it dealt itself out of the cost-of-living debate in the electorate.

Since then, the political environment in Australia has been surreal. Aided by a compliant media, both major parties have continued to promote "cost-of-living pressures" as a front-line issue (even though, in utility pricing, they gave this power away). Federal and state election campaigns have become the equivalent of a financial auction, with front-benchers trying to spin the illusion of a direct solution to the so-called living-standards problem. The low point for Labor was Rudd's promise of Grocery Watch and Fuel Watch schemes in 2007 – gimmicks which did not survive the rigours of government.

On the Coalition side, the contradictions are even worse. In 2012, its Treasury spokesperson, Joe Hockey, promised to end "the age of entitlement," sweeping away middle-class welfare payments. But in the 2013 election, Abbott campaigned on so-called cost-of-living pressures, creating new middle-class welfare such as his generous paid parental scheme. He even promised, beyond this term of parliament, to reverse Labor's means testing of the private health insurance rebate. Thus the Coalition was elected on a lie: declaring a national budget emergency but releasing social policies that add to the scale of debt and deficit.

In a thoughtful contribution in Quarterly Essay No. 48 (2012), the former Queensland Labor transport minister

Rachel Nolan highlighted the absurdity of this approach. Even though we have enjoyed twenty years of economic growth, with a large boost in disposable incomes, focus-group research by the major political parties shows living standards to be a significant issue. Even though, under a corporatised model of infrastructure delivery, the public sector has lost the ability to micro-manage household budgets, media and public expectations about the role of government are still high. The result is a political pantomime in which the actors pretend Australia is time-locked in the 1970s: families are struggling financially and politicians can do something about it, ASAP.

Nolan has belled the cat:

> governments are stuck in a no-win political argument over something which they cannot control ... And being stuck in that place means they are mired in a political quagmire of their own creation. You cannot run the country or set it on a progressive path while you're still in a political debate that should have finished fifteen years ago [following the introduction of National Competition Policy] and while you're running the day-to-day operations of a series of dense and heavy state-owned bureaucracies. The country is crying out for a clearly stated economic agenda ...

It was never intended for the Keating Settlement to provoke a low-grade public debate about the cost of living. The 1983–96 reforms were designed for "arm's length" economic management. The role of government was to oversee the framework within which various economic agents could prosper. Financial benefits for the public, such as internationally competitive tax rates, were to be a by-product of this framework, rather than orchestrated at election time as a monetary enticement. The objective was to end the McEwenite culture of preferment and questionable single-purpose expenditures.

When financial issues are dealt with at arm's length, it creates room in the daily media cycle for Labor to emphasise its other progressive reforms, such as social initiatives and action on climate change. As the experience of the Rudd and Gillard governments showed, when cost-of-living issues dominate, it is detrimental to centre-left parties. Labor struggled to give its non-economic achievements a positive profile. It was damned on both fronts: presiding over a miracle economy yet (having abandoned the Keating legacy) failing to receive electoral credit for the success of Australia's policy framework; bogged down in a living-standards debate which diverted attention from its social agenda.

At several levels, this is a debate Labor cannot win. In an electoral auction, it will always be outbid by the Coalition (which has few social-investment priorities). The debate itself overshadows the promotion of progressive ideas for service delivery and environmental protection. It also creates a problem of moral hazard: encouraging households to think if they over-extend themselves financially, the role of government is to bail them out. Once this happens, politics becomes a single-issue obsession, overrun by special pleading and bogus sob stories.

Labor in opposition would be better served by initiating a mature, factual debate about the limits of economic policy. It needs to explain to the electorate how the role of government has fundamentally changed, how cost-of-living gimmicks and promises are a campaign con-job. If governments are to be judged on their economic credentials, it should be in terms of macro-economic outcomes (for which the Gillard-Rudd government would have been re-elected). The ALP needs to talk openly about these truths, dismantling the politics of false financial expectations. I have no doubt such a campaign would be successful. In a society with higher levels of education, people don't like being told what to do, but they are still open to persuasion based on facts and rational argument.

In this task, there is a rich vein of information available. Again, NATSEM's research has exposed the myths of the living-standards debate. Given the issue's significance, the facts of the matter need to be quoted at length:

> With the exception of housing, the items most likely to be covered by cost of living stories [in the media], such as petrol, energy prices and fresh food, are not the main story. None of these items are notable areas of real expenditure growth. It is services – outsourcing such as child care or restaurant meals or investing in education through university or private school education that are the real pinch points of cost of living pressure ... Households are spending more money on discretionary expenditure and we find that even low income and pensioner households spend one in three dollars on discretionary items ...

FIGURE 1. Expenditure shares (1984, 2003–04, 2009–10), % total expenditure

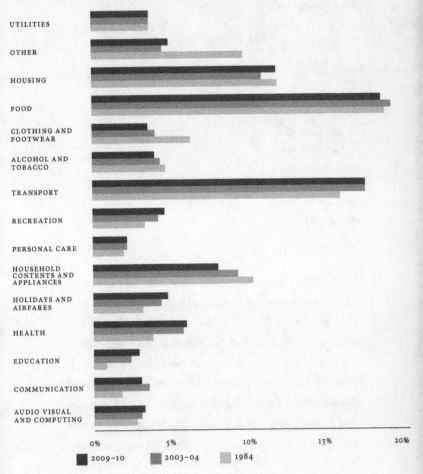

Source: ABS and Household Expenditure Survey and NATSEM.

TABLE 2. Expenditure growth
(1984 to 2009–10)

TOP 10 ITEMS	EXPENDITURE MULTIPLE
1. Tertiary education	18.7
2. Child care	11.9
3. Restaurant meals	9.7
4. Preschool/primary education	9.6
5. Sport participation	8.1
6. Secondary education	7.7
7. Other services - cars	6.8
8. Pharmaceutical products	6.3
9. Veterinary services	5.5
10. Mortgage interest	5.3

Source: ABS and NATSEM.

households [have] larger incomes and [are] spending more money on a whole range of new goods and, in particular, services that are either aspirational in nature or necessary in dealing with the demands of a modern society [such as child care to allow female workforce participation]. Focussing policy on a narrow cost of living debate around the price of electricity or petrol misses the real pressure points facing Australian households such as work/life balance and takes the spotlight off other more pressing matters that will actually help to maintain Australia's enviable standard of living for years to come.

One can imagine a Whitlam or a Keating using these conclusions with devastating effect to persuade people of the wrongness of the current debate. In fact, for Labor, cost-of-living concerns can be converted into a focus on social policy, given the large increases in household expenditure on child care and education. This is the debate the party needs to foster, instead of fluffing around with petrol bowsers and electricity meters. The ancient Labor craft of public persuasion has never been more necessary.

A REAL EDUCATION REVOLUTION

A defining feature of Rudd's first term as leader was inflated expectations. Big promises on climate change, health and education were not matched by performance in government. The much-touted revolution in schooling has been more like a Sunday church picnic than a storming of the barricades. Australia's schools today are little different from when Labor came to power in 2007.

With the release in December 2012 of international bench-marking results for Years 4 and 8 students (directed by the International Association for the Evaluation of Educational Achievement, or IAEEA), the need for education reform has become unavoidable. The data exposes Australia, measured by the standards of developed nations, as an educational backwater. We are superior to the developing nations of South-East Asia, South America and the Middle East, but struggling against the academic powerhouses of Europe, North America and North-East Asia.

In each of the five disciplines assessed (Year 4 reading, maths and science, and Year 8 maths and science) Australia was outranked by Hong Kong, Singapore, Taiwan, the United States, England, Russia and Finland. Furthermore Japan did not participate in the Year 4 reading assessment but beat

Australia in the other four areas. Germany, Denmark and the Netherlands did not undertake the Year 8 assessments but were superior to Australia in the three Year 4 tests.

In Year 4 reading, we ranked twenty-seventh out of forty-five nations. Even more disturbingly, 24 per cent of Australian students were below the intermediate benchmark standard (capable of basic reading comprehension throughout a text). In Queensland the figure was 31 per cent, in Western Australia 28 per cent and the Northern Territory 33 per cent.

In Year 4 maths, Australia placed eighteenth of fifty nations, with 30 per cent of students below the intermediate benchmark (basic knowledge in dealing with whole numbers, fractions, shapes, graphs and tables). Year 4 science produced a ranking of twenty-fifth out of fifty countries.

The Year 8 rankings, while better overall (twelfth out of forty-two nations in both maths and science), were marred by poor benchmarking results in maths. Thirty-seven per cent of Australian students lacked basic skills in dealing with decimals, percentages, graphs, tables and simple algebra. For the Northern Territory the figure was 56 per cent, Tasmania 51, South Australia 42 and Queensland 41. In four Australian jurisdictions, therefore, for every five Year 8 students, more than two found intermediate numeracy tasks beyond them. For Korea, the proportion was 7 per cent, Singapore 8, Hong Kong 11, Taiwan 12 and Japan 13. If Australia has a future in the so-called Asian century, it is certainly not in maths.

No parent could look at these results and not be deeply concerned. No serious politician, having studied the IAEEA report, could deny the need for action. The spotlight has fallen on Australia's comprehensive schools system, particularly the majority public sector. Having been involved in and studied public education for many decades, I believe the current system is adding only minimal value to students' capabilities. Most of the gains in individual learning capacity are fashioned in the home. Parents' aspirations for their children are a stronger determinant of student achievement than the institution of schooling itself.

In the conventional wisdom, schools are seen as places where children do most of their learning. Yet up to school-leaving age, children spend only a small amount of their time in school (around 10 per cent). The major role models and opportunities for education are in the home. By age three, for instance, children have acquired more than half of the language they will use for the rest of their lives. Schools, at best, are a useful addition to the learning continuum. At worst, they are places where students muddle through, making only marginal gains in knowledge and life skills.

The IAEEA findings indicate that Australian schools are muddling through. When excellence occurs, it is due primarily to home-based factors. The school learning environment is of secondary importance. How can this point be proven for Australia's student population? One way is to take a control group of pupils who have done exceptionally well and examine the factors which contributed to their success, so as to measure the relative contributions of school and family.

The selective high school system in New South Wales is ideal for this purpose. In their Year 7 intake, these schools draw on high-achieving primary school students – a case study in academic excellence. When we examine the features of this cohort (such as demographic and cultural characteristics and primary school education), one factor stands out: Asian heritage. In recent decades, coinciding with the Asian migrant intake to Australia, there has been a sharp rise in the number of selective school students from Chinese and Vietnamese backgrounds. This trend is being supplemented by the emerging success of Indian-origin students in selective entry.

Take, for example, the top twelve NSW selective schools, as measured by Year 7 entry scores in 2012. Each of them is in Sydney – a city in which 53.3 per cent of government secondary students have language backgrounds other than English (LBOTE). Yet in these leading selective schools, according to the My School website, the proportion of LBOTE pupils is 88.2 per cent, a near monopoly. The ethnic conversion rate is extraordinary: for every five LBOTE primary students there are nine LBOTE students in elite secondary education.

In explaining such a large variation, the obvious factor is the contribution of home learning. Asian parents are highly devoted to the education of their children: assisting with homework, organising extra tuition, forever encouraging excellence. In selective entry, this is their winning advantage – a family-based contribution underpinning high-level achievement. By contrast, families which adopt a "leave it to the school" approach are heavily disadvantaged. No matter which Sydney primary school they attended, pupils from a non-Asian background are less likely to attend the best government high schools.

In the public debate, we have grown accustomed to the idea of migrant families struggling to make their way in Australia. Sydney's selective school figures indicate a different trend in social mobility, with Asian parents using school-aged education as a springboard for the next generation. Their sons and daughters are moving quickly into middle-class professional jobs. The problem of immobility is greater among families from an English-speaking background, especially those on low incomes. Visit any suburban public-housing estate in Australia and this debilitating trend is obvious. The former Singaporean leader Lee Kuan Yew's prophecy about poor white trash in Australia has found a new resonance.

The statistics do not lie: comprehensive public education in Australia is struggling. It is selling short our nation's potential, both in terms of international economic competition and as a domestic social good. The recent benchmarking results will further encourage aspirational parents to move to the non-government sector. Increasingly, government schools are becoming a residual system, catering for a disproportionate share of students with learning and behavioural problems. Many families feel trapped, wanting better for their children but unable to afford private-school fees.

The crisis in public education is Labor's greatest social-policy challenge. The starting point for reform is to be honest about the failings of government-run neighbourhood schooling. The comprehensiveness of the system has dumbed down standards, levelling out classroom learning to the lowest common denominator. Large state education bureaucracies have placed a dead hand on innovation, encouraging uniformity and generating mediocrity. Public schools have become a production line for internationally substandard results, especially in the outlying states.

The measurement of classroom results and reporting of information to parents is still rudimentary. Nothing threatens vested interests inside the system more than rigorous performance measurement. It exposes bad practices and bad teachers, putting pressure on principals to do something about them. Without the discipline of measurement, students with learning difficulties are simply left behind – rationalised away as too dumb to learn and too hard to teach.

Chronic under-investment in the teaching profession has undermined the quality of tuition. Compared to knowledge workers in the new economy, Australia's teachers are shockingly underpaid. When this is combined with lax university entry requirements, teaching is no longer seen as an honoured and well-rewarded vocation. The profession is old and getting older, often with substandard teachers serving for several decades at one school and then drifting into retirement. Archaic industrial agreements have produced a sheltered workshop environment. In most states, it is impossible to get rid of under-performing staff.

This is the trade-off state governments from both sides of politics have engineered since the 1970s: low remuneration levels, offset by generous working conditions for teachers. In New South Wales, for instance, a long-serving, low-quality teacher can take six months of accumulated leave (with a relief teacher in charge of her class) and then return to the same school, having decided to work part-time. This industrial entitlement creates disruptive job-share arrangements in the classroom (with two part-time teachers). At every turn, the workplace rules have been constructed for the convenience of staff, ahead of the best interests of students.

A real education revolution involves four system-changing reforms. The first is to rebuild the teaching profession, attracting talented people who are otherwise being lost to financial opportunities in private enterprise. This involves substantial pay increases, plus the introduction of performance pay. In return, outdated work practices should be abolished. University entry standards also need to be increased (through separate interviewing and testing processes), thereby lifting the status of teaching. The profession needs to regain its standing as an elite tertiary vocation, instead of a poorly paid job for society's hard-triers.

There should be no place to hide for under-performers in government schools. The knowledge and skills of teachers need to be tested regularly, an essential discipline for an ageing profession. This information should then be reported to parents. They have the right to know about the capacity of the people instructing their children – one of the basic rights of modern citizenship.

With new rights come new responsibilities. A second reform is to ensure all parents follow the Asian example: at every opportunity, supporting the education of their children. For parents who lack literacy and numeracy skills, schools should be funded to provide remedial adult-education courses. An incentive system should also be established, rewarding parents who assist with homework and class reading programs. Principals should have the capacity (and funds) to waive excursion fees for these families (in some cases, costing up to $1000 per annum). Parents who refuse to do the right thing would continue to pay – a financial sanction on irresponsibility.

After-school tuition is one of Australia's fastest growing industries. High- and middle-income families are seeking to compensate for the failings of classroom instruction by using professional services outside school. Students from low-income backgrounds are at a comparative disadvantage. Often this is a double jeopardy: parents who do not assist with homework and do not have the funds to pay for special tutoring. Governments need to introduce a means-tested tuition voucher scheme, ensuring that poor families are not left behind in the race for academic achievement.

A striking feature of Australia's education system is the differing standards of preschool and school education. Generally, preschools are responsive, caring and highly professional facilities, with higher standards of service than schools. This is a product of their different management structures. Most preschools are community-based, with the autonomy to adapt their services to individual needs. One of the objectives of education policy should be to run schools on the successful preschools model – a third reform.

This requires the transfer of management control from state bureaucracies to principals, parents and communities. Since 2010, the Barnett government in Western Australia has been encouraging the establishment of independent public schools. These are government-funded facilities run by principals and school boards, comprising industry and community representatives. There are now 255 of these schools in Western Australia, more than one-third of the state's public education system.

This is similar to the American charter school model. Independent public schools sign up to performance agreements with the education department which are then reviewed every four to five years – ensuring that schools fulfil their charter of service delivery. Under the WA system, schools are able to select staff, manage leave and budgets and determine the curriculum which best suits their students. They often work in local and regional clusters, sharing resources and ideas for improved teaching. This is the type of system Labor needs to support nationally. With the publication of the IAEEA results, inertia is no longer an option.

The fourth reform is to create comprehensive measurement systems for Australian schools. In many respects, an education revolution is a measurement revolution – pressuring substandard schools and teachers to improve results. The National Assessment Program for Literacy and Numeracy (NAPLAN) testing and the My School website are a useful start, but more needs to be done. While the website publishes basic value-adding data (the improvement student year groups make between tests), this is not broken down class by class, allowing an assessment of the performance of classroom teachers. Nor does the website encourage competition among local schools by directly comparing their value-adding results.

Labor needs to support four major changes to school measurement:

- Conducting NAPLAN tests annually (rather than every second year) and starting them in Year 2. Currently in primary schools, NAPLAN applies to Years 3 and 5. This means, in the assessment of value-adding data, it is not possible to gauge a school's outcomes until students reach the end of Year 5. This is too late, delaying remedial action in under-performing primary schools.

- Publishing value-adding results for each class on the My School website, thereby facilitating public accountability in the performance of individual teachers. Annual end-of-year testing would make this possible.

- Providing value-adding comparisons between local schools, not only published on the My School website but also mailed directly to parents. This is the type of information parents want: a hard-headed assessment of how their school is performing relative to the other schools they know and talk about in their district.

- Surveying parents who take their children out of schools, thereby measuring dissatisfaction levels in a practical way. This should be part of the My School reporting process – identifying systemic problems (such as bullying) and forcing schools to resolve them, instead of just watching the victims transfer to other schools.

This reform program requires new government spending, especially in reconstructing the teaching profession and expanding after-school tuition. These targeted outlays are a better option for the ALP than open-ended school funding increases. Simply writing a cheque to schools is not a solution. System-wide institutional change is needed to repair the damage done to public education.

In the lead-up to the 2013 election, Labor had a major victory when Abbott and his education spokesperson, Christopher Pyne, agreed to support, over the next four years, the Gonski school funding envelope. With the consolidation of this policy, the ALP in opposition needs to focus on questions of institutional quality and incentives. The macro-funding battle has been won. The debate now needs to turn to issues of micro-reform in the school education sector.

THE NEW WAR ON POVERTY

Government school reform is a key element in breaking the intergenerational poverty cycle. Academic achievement is a poor child's passport out of a bad neighbourhood. It makes sense to put the best teachers in the worst-performing schools, offering bonuses for value-adding results. The home learning environment also needs to be targeted for special assistance. While better funding of disadvantaged schools is important, it remains a lower-order concern behind the quality of teaching and parenting. School grants can never match the benefits accruing from inspirational teaching and responsible parenting.

In the traditional left approach to welfare policy, it is assumed that disadvantaged people would be like the rest of society if they had more choices in life. Thus the poor are treated as victims of an uncaring society offering insufficient opportunity. The problem with this approach, however, is that it underestimates the importance of the social conditions in which poor people actually live. It ignores the debilitating impact of underclass culture, how welfare dependency entrenches itself in the permanent chaos of destructive behaviour: relationship problems, substance abuse and street crime.

When disadvantaged people congregate in disadvantaged places (as they do in public-housing estates and other poor neighbourhoods), it magnifies their economic and social exclusion. There is something about the place which holds people back. The neighbourhood's problems are greater than the personal characteristics of its residents. That is, if one were to examine the education levels, labour-market history and other poverty indicators for each household, they would point to a level of deprivation less than that actually experienced in the suburb. This is a problem that plagues remote indigenous townships as much as urban communities.

In practice, the residents of these areas have lots of choices, in the services available to them in the modern welfare state. They could make good use of government labour-market programs and re-enter the workforce. They could encourage learning in the home, assisting in the education of their children. They could refrain from domestic violence and stabilise their family's circumstances. And so on.

Choices are available. Ultimately, however, the problem of the underclass is an inability to make good choices in life – a blindness to the possibilities of personal change. The social norms of the neighbourhood are so badly corroded that rational behaviour becomes a minority influence, the sort of thing which strange people do. What the rest of society regards as normal is seen as socially aberrant. In effect, a subculture has formed, in which residents only mix with people from the same underclass background, sharing the same ethos of irresponsibility and hopelessness.

Not surprisingly, these values are passed on to the next generation. When young people grow up in communities with role models for work and responsibility, they tend to follow these norms as adults. Take them away and abnormal behaviour becomes a way of life. During my time as a federal MP, representing four large public-housing estates in the seat of Werriwa in south-west Sydney, one of the saddest things I heard was the principals of disadvantaged high schools talking about career counselling. When asked about their work aspirations, students would often say, "I'm going to do what my dad and granddad do – go on the dole."

Poverty alleviation is not, in the first instance, about the quality of services. It is about breaking down the culture which makes the rational use of government services improbable. It is about altering behaviour. The starting point for reform must be to change the financial incentives of welfare dependency, to use special payments as a way of breaking the underclass cycle. Amid the chaos and confusion of feral lifestyles, the one cultural norm that remains universal is an appreciation of money. It is the logical mechanism by which governments can leverage improved attitudes to work, education and community involvement. Anything which encourages the poor to regularise their behaviour is public policy gold, with long-term savings to the budget in welfare, health and law-and-order costs.

As noted above, in the schools system this means incentives for better parenting, the introduction of tuition vouchers and rewards for high-performance teaching. Elsewhere, the two interventions that make best sense are in subsidising workforce entry and geographical mobility. Offering bonus payments for the long-term unemployed to stay in new-found jobs helps to embed the cultural norms of work – a vital demonstration effect for younger generations. The longer someone stays in a job, the less likely they are to return to a no-hoper existence. Thus greater emphasis should be given to labour-market incentives, complementing punitive programs such as work-for-the-dole.

In targeting the geographic concentration of poverty, Labor should adopt a welfare strategy of dispersal. If disadvantaged people are moved out of underclass suburbs, they have a far better chance of breaking the social habits of the underclass. In public housing, where governments have the power to move tenants around, this is a straightforward task. Instead of persevering with broadacre estates – the failed sociology experiments of the 1970s – governments need to lease back private dwellings for public tenants, integrating families into "normal" neighbourhoods. Usually there is no shortage of available land in large public housing estates, making them ideal for redevelopment. Suburbs which were based entirely on public rental can be converted into a public–private housing mix.

Relocation strategies are also needed in the cause of Aboriginal welfare. Forty years of land rights reform, encouraging Aboriginal people to remain in uneconomic locations, has been a failure. It has allowed the left to believe it has done something positive for these communities when, in reality, they are still living in abysmal conditions.

Whenever I have visited remote indigenous townships, my conclusion has been: Bill Gates couldn't turn a dollar in this desolate place. What hope is there for poor people living in humpies? Historically, these tend to be places where well-intentioned missionaries moved nomadic Aboriginal tribes into Western-style townships. But instead of finding God, the locals found grog.

While the mining boom has produced jobs for some Aboriginal communities, mainly in Western Australia, most remain isolated from these opportunities. Without any reasonable hope of economic advancement, indigenous culture has collapsed into a sink-hole of drugs, alcohol and sexual abuse – the senselessness of crimes against one's self and one's kin. In practice, the spiritual affinity these communities feel for their land has been negated by the dull haze of alcoholism and other addictions.

The promise of abstinence-led solutions has failed. This is the depressingly familiar cycle of indigenous policy-making in Australia: media hype about a new Aboriginal leader and welfare reform, followed by a period of high hope and implementation, followed by muffled reports of failure, followed by frenetic excuse-making and blame. New-wave reformism has not succeeded, any more than the welfare statism of the 1970s.

After ten years of Noel Pearson's reform program in Cape York and six years of the federal government's Intervention in the Northern Territory, the results are desultory. High expectations have not been matched by tangible improvements in lifestyle normality, schooling and the development of new business ventures. The reason for this is straightforward. As long as disadvantaged Aboriginal people continue to live in isolated, disadvantaged communities, they can never break the cycle of underclass culture.

Instead of dreaming that one day Pearsonism or the Intervention might deliver progress, governments should offer financial incentives and support for Aborigines to move to places of genuine economic activity. This might not be a politically correct policy, it might not fit the mould of indigenous self-determination, but it is the only way in which practical results can be achieved. When large numbers of people are living in squalor, what matters is what works.

LIGHT-TOUCH SOCIAL DEMOCRACY

Attention to education policy and poverty alleviation will always distinguish the ALP from its conservative opponents. But what else needs to be done in making society fairer? At this point, if readers are familiar with the standard texts of social democracy, most likely you are bracing yourself for a long list of interventionist policies – each well-intentioned, each nobly designed, each trying to mould society in the image of a leftist template.

I want to suggest something different: that instead of doing more policy work, Labor needs to do less. It needs to recognise the transformation of society driven by economic growth and prosperity. Australia has been though a self-reliance revolution. With the great surge in income levels and higher education attainment, most people can do more things for themselves. They have less need for politics and, thus, less interest in politics.

Nearly 60 per cent of Australian adults now hold post-secondary qualifications, people with the skills and confidence to make their own way in the economy. And this proportion continues to grow, the beneficiaries of Labor's drive to make education and training universal. In an affluent society, families want to buy in the services that best suit their needs. It doesn't matter whether these are publicly or privately run, as long as they get the job done. With access to new information technologies, people have never been better informed (on subjects that interest them) or more articulate. Other than in heavily disadvantaged communities, feelings of powerlessness have dissipated.

It was only after I left parliament that I began to fully understand this change. MPs are trapped in a culture which emphasises problems in society. Nobody comes to electorate offices to talk about their new job and new-found prosperity. They come only with complaints. So too the commercial media specialises in a doomsday view of the world. Outside this political bubble, Australia is a very different place. The social impact of rising affluence and self-sufficiency has been phenomenal.

In terms of policy development, a turning point has been reached. In an electorate with a high degree of self-reliance, there is less work for social democrats to do. The assumptions of Whitlamism about service delivery, so enabling and enlightening in their time, are not as relevant. The great breakthrough in Whitlam's thinking in the 1960s was that the needs and aspirations of suburban Australia could only be satisfied by a bigger role for government. He ended the party's narrow focus on nationalisation and industrial relations by developing a new agenda for education, health and urban services. The best summary of his vision was in his 1969 policy speech:

We of the Labor Party have an enduring commitment to a view about society. It is this: in modern countries, opportunities for all citizens – the opportunity for a complete education, opportunity for dignity in retirement, opportunity for proper medical treatment, opportunity to share in the nation's wealth and resources, opportunity for decent housing, the opportunity for civilised conditions in our cities and our towns, opportunity to preserve and promote the natural beauty of the land – can be provided only if governments – the community itself acting through its elected representatives – will provide them. Private wealth is insufficient now to provide such opportunities even for the wealthy few. The inequalities in our community now reflect not so much gross disparities in income, but the failure of successive Liberal governments to create opportunities for the overwhelming majority of our people – the lower, modest and middle income families – opportunities which only governments can make.

For four decades, following the election of the Whitlam government, Labor has been on a long march of state-led service delivery. The Hawke and Keating governments honoured the Whitlam legacy through Medicare, national superannuation, higher school retention rates, mass university education and environmental protection. Rudd and Gillard have moved forward with DisabilityCare, Gonski school funding, paid parental leave, public housing reform and the National Broadband Network. Each of the markers of a modern, civilised, cradle-to-grave welfare state is now in place. The great man can rest easy. His work is done.

A defining feature of the recent election campaign was the Coalition's adoption of Labor's social agenda, most notably DisabilityCare, Gonski, the NBN and carbon-tax compensation (even though it plans to abolish the carbon tax). In some aspects of welfare policy, Abbott went further than the outgoing government, such as his overly generous paid parental leave scheme. As with the Fraser and Howard governments before him, the new prime minister is a gold-plated welfarist. Fraser in the end was a closet leftie, supporting greater government intervention. Howard, in his desperation to buy votes, created more middle-class welfare entitlements than any other Australian leader.

As a disciple of B.A. Santamaria, Abbott is an old-fashioned state paternalist, positioning government as a counterpoint to the excesses of free-market economics at one extreme and the growth of non-Western, non-Christian values at the other. Thus his first instincts are populist, highly susceptible to electoral and interest-group pressure for more spending. As with much of Australia's right-wing cadre, he has immersed himself in the collective institutions of party politics and parliament. Abbott's objective is not to diminish state power but to use the authority of government as a way of bringing society closer to his own beliefs.

Labor may have lost seats on 7 September, but it has won the political battle that matters most: the debate about the size and role of the public sector. Over the past forty years, the party has governed for twenty-one of them and implemented a grand social and economic reform agenda. Equilibrium has been reached in the age-old ideological struggle between the individual and government. Comprehensive welfare state services are here to stay. This should be a cause for celebration among Labor's true believers, even in this searing moment of election defeat.

What, then, is the task for the next generation of Laborites? Obviously, to preserve the gains of social democratic reform: the Keating economic model and Whitlamite service delivery. But also to recognise a new reality: in a more self-reliant electorate, the need for public sector largesse is not as great. For most citizens and communities, the private sector is no less capable of meeting their needs than the public sector.

Take the question of fiscal policy. With a 20 per cent increase in real disposable incomes, middle-class families have less need for government income support – an obvious way of returning the federal budget to surplus. Elsewhere, there is little need to expand further the responsibilities of the state. The long shopping list of social democratic programs can be shelved.

Unlike conservatives, who have no ambition greater than languidly preserving the status quo, progressives operate from a position of struggle, of trying to achieve things in a public life bigger than themselves. This has led to a distinctive reform technique: forever pushing for the introduction of new initiatives and new programs. The prevailing passion is to impose a leftist ideological mould on civil society.

A recent example of this approach is Chris Bowen's book *Hearts and Minds*. While I greatly admire his intellectual élan and commitment, by the end of Bowen's treatise my head was spinning at the vast number of proposals for micro-managing society – covering everything from the UN Millennium Goals to creating "more murals and pictures in public places." Just when we thought Labor in government had been over-burdened by micro-management, widely seen as a chaotic administration, the outgoing treasurer has invented a new generation of meddlesome policies. Bowen is one of the party's most capable thinkers, but he needs to shorten his shopping list.

Labor should now think about its role in terms of what I call "light-touch social democracy." Future governments will not need to be a whirring frenzy of activity, with senior ministers trying to juggle scores of issues simultaneously. Rather, with responsible economic policies and core social services intact, they can focus on three priorities:

- The importance of education policy through all stages of life – in particular, schools reform, early-childhood learning and access to post-secondary qualifications.
- The alleviation of poverty and the underclass – new ways of assisting the 10 per cent of Australians who have missed out on the benefits of the self-reliance revolution.
- The looming climate change disruption (on which I have more to say later in the essay).

This strategy should work to Labor's political advantage. For the next decade or so, Labor leaders will need to work overtime in rebuilding the party's reputation for sound fiscal management. After twenty years of sustained economic growth, the federal budget should be in surplus. The best way of restoring this fiscal discipline is to pare back the scale of social democratic ambition.

This is not an invitation for quietism or policy inertia, but rather a question of balance: consolidating past gains while understanding the good society now relies on a more targeted approach to public sector growth. Reformers no longer need to be here, there and everywhere, Kevin-style. Rudd was a highly skilled media performer, but as a government leader he had little sense of priorities. In trying to be all things to all people he ended up as nothing to anyone, especially among his colleagues (who saw the administrative confusion first-hand).

The post-war welfare state does not require a rolling program of reinvention. Rather, it needs selective improvement. Given the intensity and high attrition rate of modern politics, Labor MPs are likely to benefit from ring-fencing the scope of reform – working on fewer projects with greater effectiveness. It might actually be time for a cup of tea and an Iced VoVo.

Understanding equality

A light touch would also assist in avoiding the electoral sting of redistributive policies, a recurring trap for Labor over the past decade. Within our culture, we call taking from the privileged and giving to the less-privileged "fairness" – a basic definition. But for Australia's army of aspirational families, they judge their social standing not by their current position but by their (expected) future status. Thus redistributive policies threaten their expectations in life.

Under Howard and now Abbott, the conservatives (in parliament and the media) have worked out a strategy for exploiting this sentiment. They demonise redistribution as "class warfare," as if Labor is refighting the Russian Revolution. This is how the Tories responded to our relatively modest proposal in 2004 for the reallocation of school funding (the so-called hit list – a term still used today by politicians and commentators whose children attend elite private schools). More recently, the tactic was also deployed in the mining-tax controversy. Another modest redistributive Labor policy was portrayed as a threat to national prosperity and the aspirations of future mining entrepreneurs.

Labor's goal should be to lift up from the bottom, not to knock down from the top. Wise heads need to overrule old tribal emotions. I love nothing better in life than giving it to toffee-nosed, North Shore spivs, but the political utility of this approach has expired. I'm an anti-model for how to handle the elites. In any case, the lessons of the Rudd and Gillard governments have made the point clearly. Contrast the political success of the Gonski funding reforms (lifting up from the bottom) with the mining resource rent tax (levelling down from the top). Gonski is a good model for how to minimise interest-group resistance to social justice policies.

One of the reasons Labor has not noticed the use-by date on redistributive strategies is its outdated definition of equality. The traditional left-of-centre approach is to measure society's fairness through the distribution of material goods – that is, the relative share of income and wealth across classes of people. In an age of affluence, however, raw inequality statistics are less effective in explaining the spread of social and economic opportunity. The old relativities arose from circumstances in which society featured a small proportion of wealthy families and a large group of struggling wage-earners.

Now, with 90 per cent of citizens enjoying a strong degree of self-reliance, material measures of inequality have lost their potency. We shouldn't feel compelled, for instance, to increase middle incomes by 20 per cent just because high-income earners have achieved a 10 per cent increase. Both groups are participating effectively in the community, realising Labor's goal for decent living standards and widespread opportunity. The equity task is concentrated elsewhere: in addressing the challenges of the underclass.

It is in the DNA of the left to obsess about remaking the market and redistributing wealth. But redistribution among the top 90 per cent is superfluous if the group is already enjoying acceptable lifestyles. Levelling-down strategies have become a political quagmire for Labor, picking unnecessary fights with interest groups and upsetting aspirational values. I wish it wasn't so, but in practical terms, redistribution is a dead-end for the party.

We need to think of inequality differently, as a threshold test, measured by one's personal capability. That is, the skills and capacity to benefit from economic growth, to be active in the community, to enjoy good health and wellbeing. Labor's goal should be to ensure all citizens reach an acceptable threshold, lifting up the disadvantaged so that, in acts of self-reliance, they can do more things for themselves.

Amartya Sen put this case perfectly in his 1992 book, *Inequality Reexamined*. He argued for an understanding of equality as the freedom of each citizen to achieve reasonable goals in society:

> In the capability-based assessment of justice, individual claims are not to be assessed in terms of the resources or [material] goods the persons respectively hold, but by the freedoms they actually enjoy to choose the lives that they have reason to value … The "capability set" can be seen as the overall freedom a person enjoys to pursue her wellbeing.

Once the threshold test has been satisfied, there is no need for government to develop new interventionist strategies for these citizens. It can manage their needs and interests with a lighter touch, concentrating public resources on poverty alleviation.

Social mobility

A threshold approach to equality invites new ways of thinking about social-justice strategies. Traditionally, left-of-centre politics has focused on immediate income levels, through tax-transfer redistribution and union campaigns for higher wages. Both methods have achieved vital gains for working people. A progressive tax-transfer system and adequate industrial safety net are essential parts of a good society.

But now Laborites need to do more. To meet a threshold test of equality, they must consistently open up new opportunities for social mobility. This means welcoming economic change and dynamism – a different mindset, abandoning past attempts to deliver economic security by shielding workers from technological change and free trade. The siege mentality of refighting old battles ignores the many policy opportunities by which poor people can be empowered to participate in a growth economy.

Instead of looking at inequality through the prism of Gini coefficients and income bell curves, social democrats need to focus on intergenerational data measuring mobility. Conventional "snapshot" statistics dealing with national income distribution at a particular point in time are insufficient. They have nothing to say about groups gaining or losing Sen's capability set. The challenge of the self-reliance revolution is to make economic dynamism work for all citizens, to maximise the extent of income churning and mobility so that no part of society is permanently excluded from wealth creation.

Education access is the key: a sequence of early-childhood learning, quality schooling and near-universal post-secondary qualifications. Already a great deal has been achieved. We are now a far more egalitarian country than during the Menzies era, when only three out of every 100 working-age Australians had higher education qualifications. Most children grew up expecting to work in occupations little different to their parents. Over the past forty years, Labor governments have lifted the university attainment rate to 25 per cent, with a goal of reaching 40 per cent by 2020.

In 2012, the OECD reported on comparative rates of educational mobility in member nations. Australia ranked tenth out of twenty-seven countries – an encouraging performance. The odds of someone whose parents have low levels of educational attainment reaching university in Australia are 47 per cent. This compares favourably with other English-speaking nations, such as New Zealand (21 per cent), Canada (22) and the United States (29). We even ranked ahead of two Scandinavian countries, Norway (39) and Finland (43), plus most of continental Europe.

In 2011, NATSEM and the Smith Family reported on inter-generational mobility in education. They compared the qualifications of people born between 1964 and 1978 with those of their fathers (at a time when the children were fourteen years of age). This was a large cohort, but not one which had fully realised the benefits of post-secondary expansion under the Hawke-Keating and Rudd-Gillard governments. Nonetheless, the cross-currents of intergenerational mobility point to substantially improved social fairness. For the children of fathers with a tertiary qualification, 34.1 per cent failed to replicate their paternal heritage by going to university. More than 20 per cent did not get past "Year 12 or Below." Among the children of fathers who got no further than Years 11 and 12, 53.4 per cent went to university. For families in which the father had a vocational qualification, this figure was 41.5 per cent. For the children of relatively uneducated fathers ("Year 10 or Below"), 29.3 per cent achieved a university degree. While these figures are not perfect, they highlight the capacity of educational access to break down entrenched centres of disadvantage and privilege.

This should be a foundation stone for Labor's future. The party should now aim at 85 per cent post-secondary attainment (up from the current 57 per cent), continuing the expansion of university access but also revitalising the role of TAFE in providing vocational skills and adult and community education. Mass education links Labor's economic agenda with its social-justice goals. It bridges a wide range of constituencies: inner-city progressives, suburban aspirationals and underclass communities. It is also crucial in the evolution of progressive social values.

Education gives people a broader understanding of the society in which they live, fostering the habits of tolerance and respect for difference across racial and cultural boundaries. It encourages people to appreciate the circumstances of the less privileged, using reason instead of prejudice. Studies have shown how educational attainment correlates positively with support for social justice and collective solutions to problems.

This is why conservatives hate it. Earlier this year, I engaged in a few "culture war" skirmishes with one of News Limited's ideological spear-carriers, Nick Cater, following the release of his book *The Lucky Culture*. A striking feature of his thesis is the way in which it attacks higher education for fostering progressive beliefs. His solution is to wind back university access in Australia to the standard set by Keith Murray in his report to the Menzies government in 1957. As Cater explains it, only "16 per cent of the Australian population had the intellectual ability to succeed at university" – a Darwinian sifting process he supports for today's system.

In practice, this means expelling one-third of the student population (reducing university attainment from 25 per cent back to 16).

Conservatives often shroud this agenda in a concern for the "quality" of university teaching, creating a false dichotomy whereby quality can only be achieved at the expense of quantity, or public access to higher education. In his first statement as the Coalition's new education minister, Christopher Pyne said he was interested in capping university places as a way of improving quality. Labor should support universities in a way which allows quantity and quality to coexist. It must be a party of universality at all levels of the education system, forever improving intergenerational mobility.

Political cross-currents

The self-reliance revolution is important in another respect. It has transformed the nature of politics. People are less interested in the work of government because there are fewer areas in which it can do things for them. Self-sufficiency has produced a growing number of citizens who want the public sector to stay out of their lives, and to avoid the nit-picking intrusions of the nanny state.

Stripped of its self-importance and high media profile, politics has become a niche activity. The majority of people lead normal, well-balanced, family-focused lives. Political animals are an abnormal minority. A Melbourne University survey in May 2013, for instance, found that only one-third of people take a real interest in Australian politics. Polling by the Lowy Institute has recorded that among young Australians (aged between 18 and 29), less than one-half prefer democracy to other forms of government. Consistent with these findings, September's election featured high levels of public apathy, with a record number of young people failing to enrol, a record number of electors failing to vote and an increase in the number of informal votes (5.9 per cent in the House of Representatives, up from 5.6 per cent in 2010).

As the silent majority has lost interest in our democracy, it has been easier for small, well-organised groups of fanatics to dominate the system. In his excellent book *Glory Daze*, Jim Chalmers, the new Labor MP for Rankin, calls them "hyper-partisans." The signs are all around us:

- In the growth of niche parties, such as the Greens and Palmer United Party. At the recent election, several of the micro-parties elected to the Senate represent extreme right-wing ideals, stirred up by hyper-partisanship – most notably, Abbott's call for a "people's revolt" against the carbon tax.

- In the harder edge to political combat, evident in Abbott's opportunistic tactics as opposition leader. Throughout the 2010–13 parliamentary term he deliberately sought to manufacture crises, most notably in claims of economic ruin from the carbon tax and his declaration of a national budget emergency. Any reasonable attention to facts and balance has been lost in the Australian political debate. This deterioration is evident in what passes for discussion on right-wing blogs, specialising in hysterical claims, wild conspiracy theories and the vicious abuse of centre-left figures and their families.

- In the rise of media narrowcasting whereby, in a more competitive commercial market, right-wing outlets are pitching their content to a niche audience of fanatics. Much of this propaganda is in aid of corporate campaigns for tax breaks and resource exploitation. Large sections of the business community have adopted the politics of self-interested hyper-partisanship.

- In the emergence of an apparatchik class: parliamentary aspirants who are so hungry for politics that it is all they have ever done. This politics-as-lifestyle phenomenon has drained the system of its representative qualities, shrinking the parliamentary gene pool. It is now quite rare for people from a non-political background of salaried work to become major party MPs.

One of the golden rules of public life is that a vacuum is always filled. As self-reliant citizens have vacated the political arena, the space has been occupied by hyper-partisans. This is at odds with higher levels of education in the electorate. Fanaticism is a turn-off for the sensible centre, well-educated voters who expect a well-argued and rational approach to public policy. Thus with each election in Australia the level of disillusionment grows, creating even more space for hyper-partisanship – a cycle of democratic decline.

This trend has had a fascinating impact on the distribution of power in society. Old centres of institutional power –

such as parliamentary politics, trade unions and media companies – are not what they used to be. They have less influence and fewer people participating in them, a concentration of residual power. The action has moved elsewhere. Capability has dispersed to a growing group of self-sufficient citizens, people with the skills and resources to bypass traditional institutions. These are the cross-currents of a modern political economy.

For a party like Labor, it's a subversive process: how to aid the trend towards power dispersal and social mobility through the narrowing, increasingly unrepresentative forums of parliamentary democracy. Much has been made of Labor's shrinking base, with the decline in branch membership and trade union coverage. With so much interest in the ALP, the institutional narrowing of the Liberal Party has gone unnoticed.

Small-L liberalism is dead. Increasingly, those involved in conservative politics are fanatics. This tendency is clear among Liberal MPs, with the formation of three groupings:

- The hard-core "religious right," which is particularly prominent in the NSW and WA Liberal Party branches.
- Corporatist negotiators who seek to ensure Liberal economic policy looks after the interests of Liberal Party donors and corporate backers. This reflects the remnants of a McEwenite preferment culture, sure to be given new life under an Abbott government.
- A cadre of fanatics, rusted-on political obsessives, who represent the "authoritarian right" in Australian public life.

This last group is particularly interesting. It appears to have been influenced by the cultural norms of northern European politics. Here I'm thinking of names like Abetz, Brandis, Bernardi, Cormann, Bolt, Albrechtsen, Akerman, Roskam, Switzer and Weisser. This is Australia's right-wing hunting pack, a group of activists who share in common climate change denialism, a strong interest in race issues (especially concerning Muslims), a hatred of public broadcasting and a determination to police what they see as the integrity of Western cultural values.

While they claim to be libertarians, in practice they want an active role for government in enforcing their prejudices, in moulding society in the image of their ideology. Very often, they argue for dissenting points of view to be silenced. If they were true libertarians, they wouldn't be so obsessed with politics. They wouldn't be so deeply involved in collective organisations like parties, parliaments, governments and media companies.

The authoritarian right is well removed from the electoral mainstream. It is a foreign influence corrosive to Australian values, the clearest evidence yet of how the intellectual base of the Liberal Party has narrowed. As a case study into the way in which this group operates, it's instructive to examine the politics of 2012 in detail.

THE RISE OF THE AUTHORITARIAN RIGHT

Two thousand and twelve was a bumper year for the breaking of political conventions in Australia. For the first time, a national political leader was investigated and pursued for her professional conduct before winning elected office. Led by the *Australian* newspaper, a group of right-wing fanatics ran a smear campaign against Julia Gillard targeting her time working for the Slater & Gordon law firm in the early 1990s. No other prime minister has been treated this way, judged on their pre-parliamentary career rather than the traditional focus on parliamentary service.

In 2012, for the first time, a political staffer was the subject of sustained criticism from the other side of politics – a cowardly attack given that members of staff are limited in their capacity to defend themselves publicly. Right-wing commentators such as Chris Kenny, Andrew Bolt and Michael Smith laid into the prime minister's communications director, John McTernan, essentially for doing his job – that is, devising communications strategies for his employer. The hard-right in Australian politics confirmed that, in its obsessive pursuit of Labor leaders, no one is off limits.

For the first time, an Australian political party tried to manipulate and abuse the court system to cripple a democratically elected government. In December, Justice Rares ruled in the Federal Court that the sexual harassment case brought against Peter Slipper by James Ashby and his Liberal National Party backers had been politically motivated. A leading culprit was Tony Abbott's friend and candidate for Slipper's seat of Fisher, Mal Brough. Despite the adverse findings against Brough, Abbott re-endorsed him as the Coalition's candidate. In September's election, Brough was elected with a narrow margin, suffering a 2 per cent primary vote swing against the LNP.

For the first time, the grieving family of a political leader was attacked for political purposes. In September 2012, Alan Jones accused Gillard of contributing to her father's death, of ensuring he "died of shame." The instructive feature of these scarifying comments was not so much that Jones made them, but that dozens of so-called conservative commentators rallied to defend him – an example of immoral groupthink. A truly conservative response would have been to condemn Jones and move on to more edifying subjects (the way in which Malcolm Turnbull, for instance, handled the matter).

Yet for weeks, the far-right agonised over their champion's plight, inventing increasingly ludicrous defences of the broadcaster. In their final, delusional argument, Jones was positioned as a victim, supposedly suffering from "Fairfax's vilification" and an unreasonable lobbying campaign (urging companies to withdraw advertising from his 2GB radio program). This exposes one of the fallacies of right-wing ideologues: they claim to support the liberal ideals of freedom of speech but, in this and other cases, they denounce the public's freedom to object to Jones-style hate media. At 2GB itself, in a brazen act of censorship, one of the station's regular contributors, David Penberthy, was taken off air for daring to criticise Jones.

In its final form, the Jones affair highlighted the moral decline of Australian conservatism: its inability to unreservedly condemn wrongness in public life. As long as its enemies are under attack – no matter how indecently, no matter how far removed from community standards – it defends its own and rationalises away the immorality of the attack. Right-wingers claim a commitment to family values, yet when a daughter (Gillard) was accused of causing her father to die of shame, their main moral objection was to criticism of the accuser (Jones). This was an inversion of the Good Samaritan principle: Gillard had been wronged, yet the groupthink commentators (as listed in this essay's sources) looked at Jones and said, "This man needs our support."

In practice, these hard-right activists are value-free. Compared to their true political obsession (objecting to all things left-of-centre), their commitment to free speech and family values is vacuous. In the worst sense of the term, they are political animals: scragging, authoritarian types who seek to limit and control the public debate. This is the dangerous thing about fanaticism. The new right will not rest until its views are the only views remaining in the political marketplace.

The impact on the Liberal Party has been profound. The retiring Queensland Liberal senator Sue Boyce has voiced the concern of moderate MPs about the growing influence of Tea Party politics, warning, "We need to be on our guard that we don't end up going down the road that the Republicans have in the United States." The SA Liberal senator Cory Bernardi, formerly Abbott's parliamentary secretary, is using various front groups, such as David Flint's "CANdo" organisation, to establish a Tea Party presence in Australia.

Compounding these breaches of political convention in Australia in 2012, the authoritarian right continued its denigration of the world of science, attacking the concept of climate change and the work of climate scientists. Genuine conservatives would take a different approach to the issue. Given the international scientific consensus on the threat of global warming, they would recognise the legitimacy of the research findings and support government action against climate change – in effect, an insurance policy for the planet. The rise of far-right denialism has betrayed this cautionary instinct.

Usually, in our democratic system, scientists have a special place: as independent experts and advisers on technical matters beyond the know-how of parliamentarians. They provide recommendations on which governments can reliably act, knowing that scientific rigour has been applied in establishing the facts. There is no more arrogant act in public life than for a politician devoid of scientific qualifications to denigrate the research work of scientists. Consider, then, Tony Abbott's statement that "the [climate change] argument is absolute crap." One of the reasons the Coalition campaigned so furiously against Labor's carbon tax was its leader's conviction that global warming is bogus.

The key numbers man in Abbott's rise to the Liberal leadership was Senator Nick Minchin, a high-profile denialist.

Minchin is typical of the authoritarian right in his disrespect for scientific findings. Across several disciplines, he believes he knows more about science than the scientific community. Somewhat incongruously, in his dietary habits, he is a vegetarian, based on his assessment that red meat causes cancer. He is also on the public record describing the health effects of passive smoking as benign. His campaign against the scientific evidence of global warming is no less nonsensical. Despite retiring from parliament in 2011, Minchin remains a leading organiser of the Liberal Party's national right-wing faction – ensuring, among other things, its ongoing denial of man-made climate change.

Another denialist close to Abbott is the high-profile media commentator Andrew Bolt. He is an excellent case study in the misrepresentations underpinning the hard-right's approach to climate change. In his *Herald Sun* column of 1 February 2012, Bolt recycled (without attribution) material published three days earlier by David Rose in the UK newspaper *Mail on Sunday*. Thus Bolt wrote of how:

> the planet hasn't warmed for a decade, or even 15 years, according to new temperature data from Britain's Met Office. Hmm. That's not what global warming scientists predicted.

Nor was it what the Met Office had said about its research findings. On the same day as Rose's article (29 January), the Met Office issued the following statement:

Today the *Mail on Sunday* published a story written by David Rose entitled "Forget global warming – it's Cycle 25 we need to worry about."

This article includes numerous errors in the reporting of published peer reviewed science undertaken by the Met Office Hadley Centre and for Mr Rose to suggest that the latest global temperatures available show no warming in the last 15 years is entirely misleading.

Despite the Met Office having spoken to David Rose ahead of the publication of the story, he has chosen to not fully include the answers we gave him to questions around decadal projections produced by the Met Office or his belief that we have seen no warming since 1997.

For clarity ... a spokesman for the Met Office [told David Rose]:

"The projections are probabilistic in nature, and no individual forecast should be taken in isolation. Instead, several decades of data will be needed to assess the robustness of the projections.

"However, what is absolutely clear is that we have continued to see a trend of warming, with the decade of 2000–2009 being clearly the warmest in the instrumental record going back to 1850."

Bolt had so little respect for his readers that he failed to research and publish extracts from this statement. This is despite, on 30 January (that is, two days before the 1 February column), a reader posting a note to Bolt on his *Herald Sun* blog advising him of the Met Office's comments. In publicising Bolt's blog, the *Herald Sun* describes it as a chance for readers to "talk to [our] journalists." Yet Bolt claims not to have seen the 30 January posting.

In failing to report the Met Office statement in his newspaper column, Bolt either deliberately kept his readers in the dark or breached his professional duty to stay in touch with the public's comments on his blog. The net outcome was to rely on the misleading Rose interpretation, thereby deceiving the *Herald Sun*'s readers. Findings were presented, ostensibly from the Met Office, which the Met Office itself did not support. If, in similar circumstances, a left-of-centre politician had been this loose with the truth, Bolt would have been among those calling for his or her resignation.

Not surprisingly, several complaints were lodged with the Australian Press Council (the body funded by Australia's newspapers under self-regulatory provisions). On 13 December, the Press Council found against Bolt as he "needed to avoid conveying a misleading interpretation of the Met Office's own views on its data." In an act of stunning arrogance, Bolt's response was to attack the Press Council, accusing it of "abusing its power," "pushing a political agenda on to journalists," "punish[ing] conservatives," "making false allegations against me" and "sloppy research [and] a warmist bias." In September 2013, Bolt called for the Press Council to be abolished.

Even after the Council's ruling, Bolt continued to deceive his readers, writing on 3 January 2013 of "Australia's insane sacrifices to 'stop' a global warming that actually paused 16 years ago." Twelve days later, he went a step further, declaring, "The Met even predicts basically no further global warming for at least four more years, giving us a total of 20 years of no additional warming." This is simply untrue. In releasing its latest decadal forecasts in late December 2012, the Met Office said that its "forecast of continued global warming is largely driven by increasing levels of greenhouse gases." The temperature graph accompanying the release showed significant warming between 2012 and 2017.

Commenting on these projections on 8 January 2013, the Met Office outlined how:

> The latest decadal prediction suggests that global temperatures over the next five years are likely to be a little lower than predicted from the previous prediction issued in December 2011. However, both versions are consistent in predicting that we will continue to see near-record levels of global temperatures in the next few years. This means temperatures will remain well above the long-term average and we will continue to see temperatures like those which resulted in 2000–2009 being the warmest decade in the instrumental record ... Small year-to-year fluctuations such as those that we are seeing in the shorter term five year predictions are expected due to natural variability in the climate system, and have no sustained impact on the long-term warming.

These incidents are typical of the Bolt technique: an absence of original research and thoroughness; selective use of material to suit a preconceived agenda; deliberately overlooking evidence presented by scientific experts; and abusing independent third parties which seek to hold him to account. In effect, Bolt sees himself as a law unto himself. He never admits error, never concedes accountability and never strays from a formula of fabricated right-wing populism. As the Met Office affair showed, he only wants to know about the things he already believes in – an ignorant contempt for the values of learning and enlightenment.

Throughout 2013, Bolt's claims about climate change have become increasingly delusional. In April, for instance, he presented a graph (using UAH satellite data) as evidence of how "the pause in global warming continues." No intelligent person could look at these figures and see anything but a trend towards global warming. Before 1997, world temperatures were predominantly below the 1981–2010 average. After 1997, temperatures are predominantly above the thirty-year average. On the instrumental record going back to 1850, there is no precedent for temperatures of this kind, with the decade 2000–09 being the warmest on record. If one was to draw a trend line through Bolt's graph, it would slope upwards to the right, confirming warming of the order of 0.5 to 0.6 degrees across the 34-year period. At this rate, climate change will have a substantial impact on ecosystems and economic activity.

Bolt's daily blog has a prodigious volume of material, much of it recycled from his far-right colleagues and denialist websites, all of it attacking those in the public arena who believe in climate change, social democracy and generosity of spirit. His stock-in-trade is intimidation. By fanatically monitoring his ideological opponents, Bolt hopes to hector them into submission. He is, by deed and intent, a right-wing media vigilante.

This narrow, miserable existence is common among the authoritarian right. Other prominent exponents include Gerard Henderson from the Sydney Institute and Rebecca Weisser, the "Cut and Paste" compiler at the *Australian*. Instead of writing about fresh, creative policy ideas for helping people, they have dedicated themselves to a public life of intolerance – the daily practice of hunting down dissenting points of view.

This is the type of politics Abbott has cultivated as Liberal leader, by fostering a mean-spirited fringe group willing to attack democratic traditions to achieve power. It is a mistake to pigeonhole Abbott as a conservative. The party he leads is no longer John Howard's Liberal Party, but a very different creature, devoid of conservative respect for the ethics of our parliamentary system. Not only has liberalism disappeared from the Liberal Party, conservatism is also in retreat. Abbott has transformed Australian right-of-centre politics, replacing traditional Tory values with reactionary tactics and the strong-arming of institutions.

Naturally in politics, a leader's style sets the tone for his followers. Abbott's relentless negativity in trying to destroy Labor in a hung parliament has given a harsher, more fanatical edge to Australian politics, encouraging exorbitance among those who used to call themselves conservatives. This is why so many political conventions were broken in 2012: Abbott has let the far-right off the leash.

The Liberals have breached conventions before, most notably in the dismissal of the Whitlam government in 1975. For those of us who have maintained the rage, the memories of impropriety from this period are undiminished. Yet equally, it must be acknowledged, the Liberal Party displayed forms of contrition in the post-Whitlam years – conceding it would never again block supply in the Senate. Malcolm Fraser himself, perhaps out of guilt, has become a champion of left-wing causes, an outcast from the party he once led.

It is inconceivable the same fate awaits Abbott. In 2012, far from showing contrition, the intensity of his attacks increased. He finished the parliamentary year falsely accusing Prime Minister Gillard of criminal offences in the AWU matter – an unforgivable hyperbole. When Abbott breaks a convention, it stays broken. He then moves on to his next political cage-match. This is what makes Abbott and today's politics different: he's not for turning.

Another factor in the rise of the authoritarian right has been the changing nature of the commercial media. As news organisations face growing financial uncertainty and competition from new technologies, we are entering an era of narrowcasting, in which media companies are picking target political audiences and telling them what they want to hear. This is the rise of the Fox News model in Australia, evident in outlets such as 2GB and the *Australian*. Anyone who wants to attack progressive ideas and politicians has a ready-made platform and audience available to them. The hard-right clusters around these media opportunities – a natural habitat for commentators preaching to an anti-Labor constituency.

In terms of media management, the ALP can safely ignore these media outlets. They are not the type of forums open-minded, undecided voters go to for information. In content and style, they are a long way removed from the political mainstream. This is one of the delusions of the authoritarian right: a mistaken belief that suburban families are just like them.

In fact, with few exceptions, this cohort of commentators and broadcasters come from inner-city areas, with little practical understanding of suburban priorities. They are a fringe group with fringe interests in life, political insiders whose main point of contact is with other members of the political class. Even though they have never served as parliamentarians, they remain obsessed with parliamentary activity – a fanaticism few Australians share.

How to handle the authoritarian right

Labor needs to occupy the political middle ground. This is not only a policy challenge: implementing the Keating Settlement, education reform and practical measures to help families cope with social change. It is also a question of style and temperament. Many voters, especially younger, tertiary-educated people, find the far-right frightening. In the 2012 US presidential election, for instance, the harsh negativity of the Tea Party was a vote-loser for the Republicans. Ultimately, Australia's right-wing hunting pack will have a similar impact on support for the Coalition.

Nonetheless, this can be a tricky area for Labor. With the Liberal Party abandoning liberal values, it is tempting for the ALP to automatically pick up this policy agenda. Indeed, two prominent federal MPs, Chris Bowen and Andrew Leigh, have recently advocated such an approach. The problem with classical liberalism is its abstraction from modern society. With a rising number of self-reliant citizens, the need for the state protection of human rights is not as great. This has become a residual agenda, offering fine rhetorical flourishes for left-of-centre politicians but diminishing returns in the lived forums of civil society.

In their daily lives, highly skilled, capable people make their own opportunities – tangible progress in career paths and community activities, regardless of the well-intentioned provisions of government statutes and agencies. Laws conferring rights have been overtaken, in practice, by the opportunities self-sufficient people confer on themselves. Bowen and Leigh seem to have little understanding of this basic social change. Thus the language of Labor MPs can sound condescending, lecturing the public about rights and liberties which most people have gone out and achieved for themselves through education qualifications, good jobs and satisfying family lives.

Another difficulty with traditional liberalism is its open-ended nature. It tries to dispense social rights without guaranteeing a corresponding discharge of social responsibility. Past policies, such as multiculturalism, have conveyed an impression that Labor celebrates diversity for diversity's sake, without a more tangible national purpose. When some beneficiaries of multiculturalism (for example, ethnic street gangs) do the wrong thing, many voters conclude that, in implementing its policy, Labor failed to set appropriate boundaries for social behaviour. Thus well-intentioned liberalism can be an electoral liability.

It can also be counter-productive within the community. When governments pass laws to address racial discrimination, sexual prejudice and other forms of intolerance, this can actually harden public views about the intended beneficiaries. For instance, low-income white males, who think governments are not doing enough for them, may feel aggrieved that other parts of society have been targeted for assistance while (yet again) they have missed out.

Classical liberalism, with its mandating of new individual freedoms, worked best in a different era: early-twentieth-century society, when community values and social stability were stronger. As the American political scientist Alan Wolfe has argued:

> If everyone is free to act as he or she chooses, what exists to ensure people will recognize their obligations to one another? ... for most of its history liberalism did not need to answer this question. A liberal theory of politics was linked to a conservative theory of society. By simply assuming that liberal citizens were tied together morally by tradition, culture, religion, family, and locality, liberal theory was able to emphasize the benefits to be gained from the free exercise of political rights, since society could always be counted on to cement the moral obligations that politics neglected.

Such a society has now passed. The free exercise of human rights, in tandem with the changing nature of work and communication technologies, has loosed the glue of social capital.

This is the price of modernity: instead of being heavily inculcated in traditional social norms, our obligations to each other have become optional. The challenge for progressive government is to maintain the benefits of pluralism and personal freedom while encouraging solidarity among citizens.

We need to understand how liberalism has lost relevance, how it has slipped down the list of priorities for Labor. In this diminished form, if the party is to pursue remnants of the rights agenda, it should follow a program of what I call "liberal solidarity." That is, new freedoms should be counterbalanced by policies for individual responsibility and the rebuilding of communities of interest. Rights alone are not sufficient to create a good society. Having the right to do something does not always make it the right thing to do. More is needed: a collective recognition of right and wrong.

In an electorate disturbed by the anti-social behaviour of others, classical liberalism needs to be tempered by personal responsibility and an emphasis on the public good. The role of government is to leverage these outcomes, making the exercise of liberal rights conditional on ethical behaviour. Examples of this approach include:

- Balancing freedom of speech against new laws for improved standards in the media, particularly in safeguarding the privacy and dignity of citizens.
- Positioning multiculturalism as giving Australia the Asian language and business skills needed to maximise economic opportunities in the region – hence the primacy of skills-based migration.

- Promoting women's rights and equality in tandem with programs that address men's issues, such as health and self-esteem problems among older males.
- Balancing the right to free public education with the parental responsibility to assist schools and improve the home learning environment.
- Tempering the right to enjoy new communication technologies and social media with government policies to assist families with child protection and privacy concerns.
- Balancing the right to free public health care against the individual responsibility for health outcomes, especially when it comes to smoking and Australia's obesity epidemic. Patients who do not follow medical advice in the treatment of these conditions should lose part of their publicly funded entitlements.

Liberal solidarity aims to give all citizens a stake in the rights agenda, the safety net of knowing that social diversity is for a greater collective good, not the fragmentation of traditional values. Rather than treating human rights as an abstract legal question, these need to be understood through their practical impact on people. Public reassurance and acceptance are paramount. On this and other issues, Labor needs to be a party of community engagement – underscoring the importance of the organisational reforms outlined earlier in this essay.

Community engagement is not just a political strategy. It is also essential for the development of liberal solidarity. In nearly fifty years living in south-west Sydney, including seventeen years in public office, I can list the number of times people have raised abstract rights issues with me on the fingers of one hand. The bigger suburban concern is about antisocial behaviour.

This is an interesting feature of the changing face of the Labor Party: the more top-heavy it has become, having lost its local membership ballast, the more dedicated it has become to the introduction of liberal rights. The two have gone together, symbiotic in nature. Community engagement is a way of rebalancing the party, of ensuring that human-rights legislation is accompanied by new policies for personal responsibility and social solidarity.

The electorate has a lot of experience and ideas in this field. In public life, nothing beats listening to people who have encountered a problem and thought about a solution. The conversation today is about decency, respect and reconstituting the commons – the aspirations and values good citizens might share across cultural boundaries. It is insufficient for Labor MPs to announce new rights-related measures and expect the public to passively comply with this legislative template. Bowen, for instance, has written of how:

> In 2011, as Minister for Immigration, I committed the Labor government to multiculturalism as official government policy. But I made it clear that Australian multiculturalism involves responsibilities on behalf of all: that Australia would respect and celebrate the cultures of those who choose to make Australia their home, but that

where there were any inconsistency with the traditional Australian values of democracy, freedom, sexual equality and tolerance, then migrants would have the responsibility to respect the primacy of those traditional values.

This was Bowen's best attempt at marrying rights with responsibilities. I know his Western Sydney electorate of McMahon well, with its strikingly multi-ethnic population. Only a tiny fraction of his constituents would be aware of his 2011 proclamation, let alone influenced by its directives. Bowen was engaged in an act of grandiose delusion, believing a ministerial bully-pulpit could transform the values and behaviour of ethnic communities around the country. He is an example of how senior Labor figures have abstracted themselves from the real-life practice of Labor constituencies.

Whether in devising electoral strategies or developing policies, the ALP's best response to the rise of the authoritarian right is to embed itself in grassroots politics – the nation's true middle ground. The party has always been strongest when interacting with Australians outside the political class. This is the space Labor MPs need to occupy, knowing that their opponents have moved to the ugly, right-wing fringe of the national debate.

THE GREAT DISRUPTION

Global warming is the issue that can change everything. We know this from the irrational right-wing response to climate change. The Industrial Revolution created two pervasive institutions: market-based capitalism and carbon-based production. The two go together like husband and wife. An attack on one is an attack on the other.

This is how the far-right views global warming: not as a scientifically proven phenomenon, endorsed by every national scientific academy in the Western world, but as a political assault on the legitimacy of capitalism. Climate change sceptics are dangerous ideologues who, devoid of reason and intellectual substance, defend the free market at any cost. Most people see capitalism as a means towards a higher standard of living. The hard-right sees it as an end in itself.

In some cases, the sceptics are warriors left over from the Cold War. Their basic instinct is to be anti-left. When the left advocated state socialism, they were anti-communist. Now that the left is worried about global warming, they are climate change denialists. Their scepticism is not based on scientific fact and the public interest. It is not founded on rational policy-making and caution about the future of the planet. It is politics, first and foremost. The far-right is frightened that climate change might be used as a rationale for reforming or even abolishing capitalism.

Denialism comes in different forms. There are those (like Andrew Bolt) who are upfront about their politics in attacking climate scientists, in misrepresenting reports, in repeatedly seeking to obscure the facts. Then there are those (like Tony Abbott) who are more strategic, hiding behind politically motivated excuses for failing to act (the most common of which is the need to wait for an internationally binding UN agreement). Stripped of this rhetorical convenience, most Liberal and National Party MPs are climate change sceptics.

This is what makes the issue so frustrating for social democrats. Their instinct is to save capitalism from itself. The history of Labor politics is bound up in this simple proposition: civilising capitalism, not replacing it. This was the role of Keynesian economics in the Great Depression; it was the lasting achievement of the welfare state after World War II; and, in Australian politics, it was the purpose of Keating's reform program in the 1980s – doing the things to modernise the economy that the Fraser government had failed to do.

The political question arising from global warming is little different: can social democrats save capitalism from itself? Can they reduce the economy's reliance on carbon while also maintaining a profit-based economic system? Can they do what true conservatives should have done for themselves, taking out policy insurance against environmental devastation? Can they overcome the denialism and obscurantism of their opponents and, once more, prevail in civilising capitalism?

The early signs are not encouraging. Labor's experience with the introduction of a carbon tax has been traumatic. The Coalition's scare campaign gave it a clear electoral advantage, contributing to its 2013 victory. A major part of the problem, however, was Gillard's 2010 pledge of "no carbon tax under a government I lead." The broken promise did more damage electorally than cost-of-living concerns. This is a crucial lesson: in opposition the party needs to establish a definitive policy position on climate change and present it to the Australian people without equivocation.

Politically and ethically, Labor has no alternative but to continue advocating a market-based mechanism for reducing carbon emissions. It needs to regard carbon pricing as an immutable principle, no different to its support for Medicare and free public schooling. The challenge is not to crab-walk away from right-minded policy, but to crusade for a better public understanding of why the policy is right. Again, the lost Labor tradition of political persuasion is vital. This is not just a matter of explaining the facts of climate science and the threat to Australia from global warming. The cost-of-living debate also needs to be recast, as suggested earlier in this essay.

In its policy work, the ALP needs to guard against climate change programs being used as another wasteful form of industry policy. The emphasis should be on simulated markets, creating a low-carbon economy through the impact of carbon pricing and Australia's mandatory renewable-energy target. In the long history of capitalism, there is no evidence of government-led industry programs developing new technologies. Throwing public money at companies will not lead to greenhouse gas abatement. The only effective way of stimulating alternative energy sources and corporate investment is through a pricing imperative. In the usual pattern of market economics, a scarcity of supply drives up prices, encouraging innovation and the development of substitutable goods.

From a financial perspective, global warming is an artificial problem. The world has an abundant supply of fossil fuels, offering little incentive for the development of new forms of clean energy. This is why governments need to act through mandated pricing mechanisms. The experience throughout the Western world, however, has been disappointing. Few governments have set a high carbon price. Even Australia's scheme, setting aside the political and media hyperbole, is quite mild. It has no ambition to change consumer behaviour – in fact, due to its generous compensation scheme, most families are better off financially. They now have more money to spend on carbon-intensive products than ever before.

This is the prisoner's dilemma in international climate change policy. For electoral reasons, governments in the Western democracies are reluctant to act. For developing nations, the issue is more fundamental: securing the same carbon-laden path to economic development which rich countries have enjoyed. An effective global agreement on climate change is unlikely. Few players will move because most players believe no one else is moving.

The conflict between rich and poor nations was outlined graphically by Andrew Charlton in *Man-Made World*, Quarterly Essay 44. In his role as Kevin Rudd's economic adviser, Charlton was an Australian representative to the 2009

Copenhagen conference. He noted how developing countries, while concerned about climate change, saw poverty as a bigger problem. "For centuries, your countries have prospered by exploiting the world's resources," a Latin American negotiator lamented: "How can I tell the slum dwellers they must stay poor to clean up your mess?"

For Charlton:

> This was the conundrum in Copenhagen. A fraction of the world's people had become rich by plundering our planet to the point of exhaustion; now the still-poor majority wanted to do the same. "We shouldn't be too hard on ourselves," a German colleague said to me. "We have to be realistic about the problem. The world is split between those who want to save the planet and those who want to save themselves."

Most likely, the global political system is marching into the folly of disastrous global warming. The predicted damage is well known: the loss of valuable ecosystems and arable land, with major disruptions to economic and social activity. Lower crop yields, especially in developing nations, will add to the spread of global hunger and poverty. Rising sea levels will damage a range of industries and threaten the interests of home owners and coastal communities. The unpredictability of weather events is also likely to increase, adding to the human and financial cost of natural disasters.

Less clear is the likely political response to these problems. In recent decades, there have been two grand theories for charting the destiny of Western civilisation. The first was Francis Fukuyama's *The End of History and the Last Man* (1992), a Hegelian thesis on the permanent triumph of liberal democracy – man's "natural" state. The second was Samuel Huntington's *The Clash of Civilizations and the Remaking of World Order* (1996), an argument that the driver of world history will no longer be economic or ideological, but cultural. Following September 11, Huntington's work has offered a framework for the conflict between Western and Islamic civilisations.

A third scenario should be added to this list: the impending climate change disruption. The role of centre-left parties will be to mediate the political and institutional tensions in society, to manage a governmental response to the crisis. In these circumstances, the far-right will be discredited politically, the fraud of denialism weakening its credibility. At the other extreme, far-left parties such as the Greens, with their dogmatic approach to issues, are unlikely to play a realistic role in reconciling the competing interests of capital, labour and the environment.

Perhaps the best comparison is with the Great Depression. During the 1930s, the right had little to offer in the way of solutions. Left-wing movements became more popular but, in practice, were unable to ameliorate the economic collapse. It was left to social democrats to implement financial reform and develop a new social safety net – a practical, mediating role in the political economy of Western nations.

It is not possible to know precisely how climate change disruption will develop, but some assumptions can be made.

Later this century, Australian Labor is likely to confront circumstances in which:

- Economic output and income levels will be reduced by the impact of global warming.
- The values of a consumerist society, relying on carbon-based materialism, will be inappropriate for dealing with the disruption.
- Concern about the natural environment will be the leading political priority.
- Carbon pricing will become an orthodox, common-sense approach for reducing greenhouse-gas emissions.
- No policy option can be ruled out, with renewed legitimacy for the idea of government intervention to overcome the crisis.
- Tensions between affluent and developing nations will increase, as the blame game for climate change intensifies.
- Internationalism will be vital, with social democrats everywhere needing to cooperate in finding solutions.

For 150 years before the fall of the Berlin Wall, left theorists wasted their time with the ideological dead-end of state socialism. Now history looks like giving them a chance at redemption. The priority for progressive thinkers must be to prepare for the great climate disruption. More than any other factor, this will determine the long-term future of left politics.

The ALP needs to be part of this effort. It needs to campaign continuously on global warming: combating scepticism, explaining the difference between weather events and climate trends, drawing attention to the findings of climate scientists and preparing the electorate for change, both in the world's environment and the nation's political economy. It cannot afford to be permanently bruised by the carbon tax experience.

In effect, in coming decades, Labor has an educative role. One of the consequences of a better-educated society is that people have become more self-assured in their use of information. In knowing so much themselves, they are more cautious about the big, sweeping claims of others. In the Information Age, it seems, everyone is a master of every subject they hear something about.

This is a feature of the climate change debate. Confident, middle-class citizens who know a lot about weather events also see themselves as climate experts. The findings of climate scientists are not accepted automatically or deferentially. This is not a crude, ignorant dismissal of expertise (like that of the far-right denialists) but, rather, an empirical approach to knowledge. In practical suburban Australia, people rely on the things they see around them as a way of gauging the future – hence, in thinking about climate change, they are influenced by weather patterns.

Six years ago, at the beginning of this debate, Australia's drought conditions were seen as synonymous with global warming. It was a simple equation: dryness equals heat. In the 2010–11 and 2011–12 summers, however, heavy rainfall and flooding on Australia's east coast changed perceptions about climate change. Wetness equalled coolness. Now, with high temperatures throughout 2013, including an early start to the bushfire season in spring, the pendulum of public opinion is likely to swing back.

Labor should recommence its campaign on the public importance of global warming. To be mute on this subject in opposition would be a failure of leadership. To take a longer view, election results come and go, but the climate change dilemma is permanent. The worse thing we could do is get on the wrong side of history, for Labor to join the Coalition in taking an anti-science, anti-rational, anti-environment stance. Inevitably, Abbott and his band of flat-earth denialists will be condemned by the facts of climate science. The day Australians elected a denialist as their prime minister will be viewed as a day of national humiliation, an atrocity against good public policy. The ALP has enough problems to confront without mimicking the lunacy of the Liberal Party on global warming.

A POST-LEFT FUTURE

As Christmas dinners go, this one has been quite productive. Labor's membership and identity crises can be resolved. There is no political trickery or spin required. It involves understanding the party structures and policies which have worked well in the past, and giving them new relevance. The community engagement of the great Labor leaders can be reignited through primary pre-selections. This and other reforms to democratise the party will have the considerable side-benefit of putting caucus's sub-factional warlords out of business. The alternative is more of the same: a union-run oligarchy which narrows Labor's base and disconnects the party from large non-union constituencies. The underlying slippage in the party's primary vote will continue unchecked.

In reconceiving its identity, the ALP needs to answer two basic questions. Which parts of society does it seek to represent? What are its burning passions and ideas for these community interests? Recapturing the Keating economic legacy would help Labor appeal to the new aspirational class, the electoral majority the party created in the 1980s and '90s. The record of economic openness and micro-reform in Australia shows that the twin goals of growth and income fairness – efficiency and equity – can coexist. Labor's burning passions should be for education reform and poverty alleviation – new ways of giving all Australians a stake in the growth economy.

A post-left future cannot rely on the mass membership institutions of the Industrial Age: trade unionism, working-class solidarity and public meetings. Rather, inside the ALP, union leaders need to find the maturity and perspective to understand they can no longer dominate the party, accepting the need for major organisational reform. By necessity, post-left parties are smaller and more adaptable, applying a lighter touch to their policy agenda. They need to work harder to stay connected to community aspirations and to solve issues of public concern.

If Labor makes these changes, it has a future, especially given the rise of the authoritarian right. This ugly side of Australian politics is an electoral gift to a creative, sensible party of the centre-left. Most significantly, Labor is on the right side of history in the climate change debate. The logical way to approach Australian politics in the twenty-first century is through a two-phase strategy: in the short term, re-establishing the party's dominance in economic and social policy, while in the longer term, preparing for the transformative impact of global warming.

This is classic Fabianism, waiting for the right time to strike. Reports of the end of Labor history are premature. Given the probability of major climate change disruption, the most engaging chapter is yet to be written.

SOURCES

6   "Labor historian Troy Bramston has chronicled the collapse":
    Troy Bramston, "Troglodyte club refuses to reform," *The Austra-
    lian*, 5 December 2011.

9   "Contested union ballots, like attendances at union meetings":
    Rodney Cavalier, *Power Crisis: The Self-Destruction of a State
    Labor Party*, Cambridge University Press, Melbourne, 2010, p. 32.

14 "an increase in real disposable income of 11.9 per cent": AMP-
    NATSEM, *Prices These Days: The Cost of Living in Australia*,
    Income and Wealth Report, Issue 31, May 2012, p. 21.

25 "Hawke put the argument perfectly": "Dump unions, keep Gil-
    lard, says Hawke," *Australian Financial Review*, 3 January 2012.

26 "the role of 'a tiny coterie of self-interested factional warriors'":
    John Faulkner, "Political Integrity: The Parliament, the Public
    Service and the Parties," speech to the Integrity in Government
    Conference, University of Melbourne Law School, 4 December
    2012.

26 "A key conclusion of the 2010 party review": John Faulkner, Steve
    Bracks and Bob Carr, *ALP 2010 National Review*, Report to the
    ALP National Executive, February 2011, p. 26.

27 "Faulkner has criticised a system": Faulkner, "Political Integrity"
    speech.

28 "Factional binding is inherently undemocratic": Faulkner, "Politi-
    cal Integrity" speech.

31 "a policy weakness from which the party is yet to recover": For an
    outline of Labor's policy compromises in opposition (accommo-
    dating Robertson and the left) which led to the failure of its border
    protection policies in government, see Mark Latham, "Sinking
    feeling for Labor," *Australian Financial Review*, 5 July 2012.

31   "Dastyari declared": "Abolish Labor factions, says party elder John Faulkner," *The Australian*, 5 December 2012.

32   "341 party members and 3612 community voters": Approximate figures, supplied by ballot scrutineers to *Crikey*, 4 June 2012. It should be noted that a primary pre-selection trial in the Victorian state seat of Kilsyth (in outer eastern Melbourne) in April 2010 yielded a much lower level of participation, with just 40 ALP members and 136 community members voting.

33   "the young Curtin crusading for social justice": See David Day, *John Curtin: A Life*, HarperCollins, Sydney, 1999, pp. 52–6.

33   "Ben Chifley, Gough Whitlam and Paul Keating": The local political backgrounds of Chifley and Whitlam are well known. For Keating's experience, see Edna Carew, *Keating: A Biography*, Allen & Unwin, Sydney, 1988, pp. 9–12.

36   "these ideas are set out in the Faulkner/Bracks/Carr report": The 2011 Labor national conference failed to adopt any of these recommendations in full. The Faulkner/Bracks/Carr report also recommended the introduction of primary pre-selections in lower-house seats without sitting Labor members, "comprising a 60 per cent [voting] component drawn from local party members, 20 per cent from members participating from affiliated trade unions and 20 per cent from registered Labor supporters in the community." The one-fifth union component was an attempt to secure the support of union/faction powerbrokers for the proposal. The reduction of community voters to just one-fifth of the voting weight, however, is unsatisfactory – it would hardly be worth their while. The Dastyari model of 50 per cent branch members, 50 per cent general public is preferable.

43   "Meeting the right people in the Labor Party": Graham Richardson, *Whatever It Takes*, Bantam Books, Sydney, 1994, p. 12.

52   "A particularly surprising result": AMP.NATSEM, *Prices These Days*, p. 21.

54   "Keating's role was paramount": Indeed, NATSEM's figures for 2003–04 to 2009–10 (a Howard/Rudd period) indicate backsliding on income equality (see *Prices These Days*, p. 21). For each quintile, real incomes increased as follows: Q1 (low) 10.7 per cent,

Q2 14.7, Q3 14.2, Q4 17.8 and Q5 (high) 27.4. In terms of economic inclusiveness, the most impressive figures were recorded during the period of Keating's reform program and its immediate aftermath.

54 "'Labor Buries Keating'": See Troy Bramston, *Looking for the Light on the Hill*, Scribe Publications, Melbourne, 2011, pp. 82–3. The article reported that Simon Crean "is espousing intervention [in the economy] at all levels and talking of initiatives involving individual firms, specific industries and the entire economy."

55 "the great neoliberal experiment of the past thirty years has failed": Kevin Rudd, "The Global Financial Crisis," *The Monthly*, February 2009, pp. 20–29.

55 "average prices for footwear and clothing": AMP.NATSEM, *Prices These Days*, pp. 7–8.

56 "The second essay, by the treasurer, Wayne Swan": Wayne Swan, "The 0.01 Per Cent: The Rising Influence of Vested Interests in Australia," *The Monthly*, March 2012, pp. 20–24.

56 "'the Money Power'": See Peter Love, *Labour and the Money Power: Australian Labour Populism, 1890–1950*, Melbourne University Press, Melbourne, 1984.

63 "gimmicks which did not survive the rigours of government": Although, in fairness to Rudd, my "ease the squeeze" rhetoric in the 2004 election campaign was hardly any better.

64 "governments are stuck in a no-win political argument": See the correspondence section, Quarterly Essay 48, 2012, pp. 103–6.

66 "With the exception of housing": AMP.NATSEM, *Prices These Days*, pp. 25 and 31.

70 "The data exposes Australia": The full results can be found at www.acer.edu.au/timss/.

72 "children have acquired more than half of the language": See Mark Latham, *What Did You Learn Today? Creating an Education Revolution*, Allen & Unwin, Sydney, 2001, p. 87.

73 "one factor stands out: Asian heritage": See Anna Patty and Andrew Stevenson, "Migrant pupils top the entry tests for selective schools," *The Sydney Morning Herald*, 3 July 2010, particularly their conclusion that "the percentage of students from

migrant families entering the selective system has risen dramatically … the component is sharply skewed towards children from
Asian-origin families." These findings are supported by anec-
dotal evidence in speaking to parents and teachers from selective
high schools in Sydney. While the NSW Department of Education and Communities does not publish statistics for specific ethnic or language groups in selective schools, the rising success of
Chinese-, Vietnamese- and Indian-Australian families is evident
in the school community. Also, the writer Alice Pung, from a
Cambodian-Chinese background, set out a detailed account of
the impact of Asian parenting in the Victorian education system
(including selective school entry) in *The Monthly*, February 2013.

73 "the proportion of LBOTE pupils is 88.2 per cent": Measured as
an average for Baulkham Hills, Fort Street, Girraween, Hornsby
Girls, Hurlstone Agricultural, James Ruse Agricultural, Nor-
manhurst Boys, North Sydney Boys, North Sydney Girls, St
George Girls, Sydney Boys and Sydney Girls high schools. Note
that among the 11,072 students at these selective schools in 2011,
none were from an indigenous background.

75 "The profession is old and getting older": For instance, NSW
Department of Education and Communities figures (*Key Statistics
and Information 2012*) show that in March 2012, 43.5 per cent of
NSW teachers were fifty years or older. By far the biggest age/gen-
der grouping (24.7 per cent of teachers) was women aged 50–59.

79 "four major changes to school measurement": Some of these
measurement proposals were first advanced in my *Australian
Financial Review* column on 23 February 2012.

82 "point to a level of deprivation": See Boyd Hunter, "Is There an
Australian Underclass?" *Urban Futures*, No. 18, 1995, p. 20. This
argument was also advanced in my article on the Claymore
public-housing estate and Aboriginal welfare reform in the
Weekend Australian Financial Review, 6–7 October 2012, p. 49.

84 "a public–private housing mix": For an example of a successful
public housing redevelopment, see my report on the Minto estate
in south-west Sydney in the *Weekend Australian Financial
Review*, 6–7 October 2012, p. 49.

96 "In the capability-based assessment of justice": Amartya Sen, *Inequality Reexamined*, Clarendon Press, Oxford, 1992, pp. 81 and 150.

98 "Australia ranked tenth out of twenty-seven countries": OECD, *OECD Indicators: Education at a Glance 2012*, Paris, September 2012, pp. 111–12.

98 "For the children of fathers with a tertiary qualification": The Smith Family, *Unequal Opportunities: Life Chances for Children in the "Lucky Country,"* Sydney, 2011, pp. 15–17.

99 "16 per cent of the Australian population": Nick Cater, *The Lucky Culture and the Rise of an Australian Ruling Class*, HarperCollins, Sydney, 2013, pp. 229–48.

100 "only one-third of people take a real interest in Australian politics": Centre for Advancing Journalism, University of Melbourne, "Citizens' Agenda: National Survey of Voters," caj.unimelb.edu.au/research/citizens-agenda.

101 "less than one-half prefer democracy": Fergus Hanson, "The Lowy Institute Poll 2012: Public Opinion and Foreign Policy," lowyinstitute.org/publications/lowy-institute-poll-2012.

101 "Jim Chalmers … calls them 'hyper-partisans'": Jim Chalmers, *Glory Daze*, Melbourne University Press, Melbourne, 2013, pp. 99–168.

102 "vicious abuse of centre-left figures": see michaelsmithnews.com and blogs.news.com.au/heraldsun/andrewbolt.

102 "the distribution of power in society": see Moisés Naím, *The End of Power*, Basic Books, New York, 2013.

105 "No other prime minister has been treated this way": On 22 August 2012 in the *Australian*, Paul Kelly wrote of how the AWU matter was one of the "character tests applied relentlessly to prime ministers in the past and there is no reason Gillard should be granted immunity. It is absurd to pretend there is no public interest simply because the test is not about criminal behaviour." I then rang Kelly and asked if he could name any federal MP who has suffered from media scrutiny and investigations into their professional work (other than for criminal behaviour) prior to entering parliament. He replied, "I'm sure I can if I can take it on

notice." He never got back to me. Subsequently on a Sky News program, I raised the matter again. Kelly mentioned John Howard, concerning a scandal which arose in the 1990s (moonlighting as an industrial-relations consultant for Clayton Utz) when Howard was a serving MP. The treatment of Gillard is unprecedented. More generally, to understand the lies, misrepresentations and vicious libels against Gillard in the ancient AWU matter, see commentator Michael Smith's website (www.michael-smithnews.com). On 22 November 2012, for instance, Smith posted material lamenting the failure of Taliban snipers to assassinate Gillard on one of her recent trips to Afghanistan. Hedley Thomas at the *Australian* and Andrew Bolt at the *Herald Sun* regard Smith as a reliable source of information on Gillard and the AWU – another sign of how badly the standards of Australian conservatism have deteriorated.

105 "no one is off limits": See, for example, Chris Kenny, "Our egalitarianism silences the class warfare guns of Labor's spinner-in-chief," *The Australian*, 20 October 2012.

106 "increasingly ludicrous defences of the broadcaster": The campaign in defence of Jones took many extraordinary forms. For instance, Andrew Bolt (*Andrew Bolt Blog*, *Herald Sun*, 1 October 2012), Janet Albrechtsen (*The Australian*, 3 October 2012), Paul Kelly (*The Australian*, 3 October 2012), Gerard Henderson (*Sydney Morning Herald*, 9 October 2012), Tom Switzer (*The Australian*, 8 October 2012) and Neil Brown (*Spectator Australia*, 6 October 2012), among others, argued a weak position of moral relativism: that, over the years, Labor people have also said some offensive things. A second defence, as mounted by Rowan Dean (*Spectator Australia*, 13 October 2012), John Roskam (*Australian Financial Review*, 12 October 2012) and Errol Simper (*The Australian*, 8 October 2012), was that people were overreacting, that Jones's comments were not that exceptional. Dean reckoned Jones "was attempting to be amusing," while Roskam downplayed the slur as "a one-sentence comment about the Prime Minister from a radio host at a private function." For Simper, "Jones's remarks might, just, have squeaked over the line as cruel,

dark, adult satire." A third defence, as presented by Nick Cater (*The Australian*, 8 October 2012), was to excuse Jones because he does well in the radio ratings. Finally, Nick Leys (*The Australian*, 10 October 2012), Gerard Henderson (*Sydney Morning Herald*, 9 October 2012), Jennifer Hewett (*Australian Financial Review*, 9 October 2012), Piers Akerman (*Daily Telegraph*, 31 October 2012) and Paul Sheehan (*Sydney Morning Herald*, 31 October 2012), among others, positioned Jones as a victim of left-wing social-media campaigners, while Andrew Bolt (*Andrew Bolt Blog*, *Herald Sun*, 1 October 2012) claimed that Fairfax newspapers were vilifying Jones "by carefully selected photographs of the most unflattering kind." We are not talking about Clark Gable here. Even Jones's friends would acknowledge he is a bald, moon-faced, elderly person. Three of the six photos cited by Bolt were actually quite flattering of Jones. This is a measure of Bolt's delusional bias: he looks at Alan Jones and sees Orlando Bloom.

107 "taken off air for daring to criticise Jones": In a telling example, the authoritarian right was silent on Penberthy's axing as a contributor to the Steve Price/Andrew Bolt program at 2GB. As Penberthy noted on 10 October 2012, "Just over an hour ago I got a call from 2GB saying that I am no longer welcome on the network. The reason: [my] column from last Tuesday which was critical of Alan Jones." This act of censorship had no impact on Bolt, who has continued with the program, knowing that it involves the suppression of free speech. Apparently, for Bolt, censorship only matters when it happens to him – a self-serving position. To my knowledge, no right-wing think-tank, media outlet or commentator has campaigned for Penberthy's reinstatement.

107 "'we need to be on our guard'": See Phillip Coorey, "Coalition slipping to right, says Liberal senator," *Sydney Morning Herald*, 9 October 2012.

108 "'the [climate change] argument is absolute crap'": *The Australian*, 12 December 2009.

109 "The planet hasn't warmed for a decade": Andrew Bolt, "Time that climate alarmists fessed up," *Herald Sun*, 1 February 2012. The trick in the Rose/Bolt claim can be seen in Bolt's *Herald Sun*

blog for 30 January 2012. A reader drew Bolt's attention to the original Met Office data (released on 4 January 2012). Using a baseline of the long-term global average temperature (14 degrees Celsius, 1961–90), it ranked recent years for their variation above this mark (using the HadCRUT3 Anomaly measure – Met Office and University of East Anglia). Thus 1998 ranked first (0.52 anomaly, or 14.52 degrees global average temperature) and 2010 second (0.50 and 14.50), while 1997 and 2011 ranked equal bottom (0.36 and 14.36). All years displayed warming above the long-term average. Yet, in a dishonest act of statistical cherry-picking, Rose and Bolt focused on just the 1997 and 2011 figures, arguing "the planet has not warmed for the past 15 years." Global warming is not a linear progression. Average annual temperatures go up and down with natural weather variations. The only valid way of assessing climate change is through long-term trends – that is, measuring climate, not annual weather events. By comparing statistically convenient twelve-month periods in isolation, Rose and Bolt failed to do this. It should be noted that, in the original data release, a spokesperson for the Met Office explained that "while 2010 was a record warm year, in 2011 we saw a very strong La Nina which can temporarily cool global temperatures. The La Nina has returned and although it is not as strong as early last year, it is still expected to influence temperatures in the year ahead." The Met Office has continued to argue in favour of "evidence to support climate predictions which show the planet is now locked into at least two degree Celsius warming, and rapid reductions in greenhouse gas emissions are required to ensure this does not rise further for future generations." Despite this information being available via a reader comment on his blog, Bolt proceeded with his misleading 1 February newspaper article – a measure of his nefarious approach to climate change.

111 "a misleading interpretation of the Met Office's own views": Australian Press Council Adjudication No. 1558, Ellett and Others/ Herald Sun (December 2012). The Council also found that, "In a blog posting two days earlier, 30 January, [Bolt] had quoted Mr Rose's assertion about the lack of warming and a reader then

posted a comment referring him to the Met Office's description
of that assertion. The Met Office description should have been
mentioned in Mr Bolt's print article and blog of 1 February." At
this point, Bolt faced a logistical problem: if he continued to personally moderate and publish reader comments correcting his
misrepresentations, organisations like the Press Council could
use this process to hold him to account – knowing for certain he
had seen the corrective statements. So on Australia Day 2013,
Bolt announced his solution: "After campaigns against me –
exploiting restrictions on free speech – it has been deemed safer
that I not moderate [blog comments] myself. So I shall do my
best to read your comments, but they will not be published."
That is, to avoid accountability on climate change and other subjects, Bolt decided only to publish comments moderated by paid
Herald Sun staff. When these staffers are not available (such as
on weekends and public holidays), Bolt himself will not get
involved. This way, for Bolt, ignorance is bliss, ensuring that no
one can ever know which comments he has actually read. This
tactic, however, restricts the free speech of his readers – the
chance for their views to be published on weekends etc. Far from
defending personal liberty in Australia, Bolt has become a censor
of free speech. The only freedom of speech he genuinely defends
is his own.

111 "Bolt's response was to attack the Press Council": Andrew Bolt,
"I'll fight for free speech," *Herald Sun*, 15 December 2012. This is
a pattern among News Limited publications: attacking the
adverse findings of the independent Press Council, rather than
improving their journalistic standards. It makes a mockery of
the self-regulatory system, highlighting the need for statutory
regulation.

111 "Australia's insane sacrifices": See *Andrew Bolt Blog, Herald Sun*,
3 January 2013. On climate change, Bolt piles misrepresentations
on top of misrepresentations. The reference to a sixteen-year
pause (as opposed to his initial claim of fifteen years) is an
attempt to imply an absence of warming in 2012. Note that,
according to preliminary data released on 28 November, the

HadCRUT4 figure for 2012 was 0.44 – that is, 0.08 degrees higher than in 2011. Even by the terms of Bolt's own dubious methodology, warming occurred. Note also the Met Office's release on 20 December 2012 of its global temperature forecast for 2013: 0.57 degrees warmer than the long-term average of 14.0 (and 0.21 degrees higher than 2011). Anyone relying on Bolt for an understanding of climate change is bound to be misled.

111 "The Met even predicts": See *Andrew Bolt Blog, Herald Sun*, 15 January 2013, which was linked to a misleading report in the *Mail Online* from 8 January 2013. There is no limit to Bolt's mendacity. He has learnt nothing from the Press Council's ruling. He is still relying on erroneous second-hand reports, instead of checking first-hand on what the Met Office has said about its own research.

112 "The latest decadal prediction": Met Office, "Updates to our decadal forecast," press release, 8 January 2013, at www.metoffice.gov.uk.

113 "In April, for instance, he presented a graph": See *Andrew Bolt Blog, Herald Sun*, 3 April 2013, blogs.news.com.au/heraldsun/andrewbolt/index.php/heraldsun/comments/waiting_for_warming.

113 "a right-wing media vigilante": Bolt fits perfectly the Churchillian definition of a fanatic, as "one who can't change his mind and won't change the subject." For an example of his vigilante activities, visit the Radio 2GB website and listen to his discussion with Steve Price on 3 December 2012. Mid-program, when attacking Professor Andy Pitman, a climate change expert from the University of NSW, Bolt's voice changed to a weird, demented pitch. "I hope he's listening, hello to you, Andy," Bolt, in stalker mode, intoned. "I'm on to you, Andy, I'm on to you."

114 "a public life of intolerance": The vigilantes are highly dedicated but not overly intelligent. Henderson, in particular, is error-prone. For instance, he does not know the name of Tony Abbott's electorate (Warringah, not Mackellar), nor the parliamentary chamber in which Barry O'Farrell sits (NSW Legislative Assembly, not Legislative Council). He has also (falsely) implicated Malcolm Fraser (born 1930) in an (alleged) sexual relationship between Betty Fairfax (born 1907) and Bob Menzies (born 1894).

If Henderson cannot get basic facts right about Liberal leaders such as these, how accurate can he be in writing about the Labor Party? Much like Bolt, he consistently invents claims, with no regard for evidence or matters of fact. An extensive (but not exhaustive) list of Henderson's errors is set out in my *Henderson Watch* series (2011–13) in *Crikey*.

115 "an unforgivable hyperbole": One of Abbott's character traits is habitual exaggeration – see my correspondence in Quarterly Essay 48, 2012, pp. 89–91. In the AWU matter, speaking on the Channel Nine *Today* program on 29 November 2012, Abbott falsely accused Gillard of having misled the Western Australian Corporate Affairs Commissioner in the early 1990s. "Plainly on the documented evidence of the unredacted transcript she gave false information to the West Australian authorities," Abbott told *Today*. "Now for a legal partner, for a senior lawyer, to make false claims to an important statutory body like this is a very, very serious matter. It's in breach of the law." In fact, Gillard's advice to the WA authorities (that the AWU Workplace Reform Association was not a trade union) was accurate. No law had been breached. No offence had been committed.

116 "this cohort of commentators and broadcasters": My favourite example of an out-of-touch media platform is the *Australian*. In its editorial on 21 November 2012 it declared: "Politicians, bureaucrats, academics and, dare we say it, public broadcasters need to be in and of the communities they seek to serve. There is nothing wrong with a good Belgian beer. But it is amazing what good sense you might hear over a VB or two." Yet, to take one example, Rebecca Weisser's CV lists her background as living "in a squat in London and a cave in Granada, Spain." She now "lives in Sydney which she navigates on a folding bicycle" – undoubtedly while balancing a VB on the handlebars. Or perhaps the Spanish cavemen had a slab or two on ice. The *Australian* has deluded itself into believing it is embedded in a community for which, in reality, few of its staff has any understanding.

116 "recently advocated such an approach": Andrew Leigh, "On Labor and Liberalism," speech to the Per Capita Reform Agenda

Series, Melbourne, 5 December 2012; Chris Bowen, *Hearts and Minds: A Blueprint for Modern Labor*, Melbourne University Publishing, Melbourne, 2013.

118 "If everyone is free to act": Alan Wolfe, *Whose Keeper? Social Science and Moral Obligation*, University of California Press, Berkeley, 1989, p. 108.

121 "In 2011, as Minister for Immigration": Bowen, p. 21.

124 "most Liberal and National Party MPs are climate change sceptics": The Coalition's "direct action" program is an electoral fig-leaf, designed to make it appear reasonable on the question of climate change. The policy is flawed from first principles: the more greenhouse gases big-polluting companies emit, the more "direct action" Australian taxpayers would need to finance. Instead of relying on market forces to reduce carbon emissions, Abbott has invented a new government-directed program, wasting $3.2 billion on discredited carbon capture and sequestration technology.

125 "Throwing public money at companies": For a critique of the Gillard government's $10 billion Clean Energy Finance Corporation, see my column in the *Australian Financial Review*, 26 April 2012. Note that the mandatory renewable energy target requires that 20 per cent of Australia's electricity be produced from renewable energy sources by 2020. Like the carbon tax, it relies on a quasi-pricing mechanism, with the establishment of markets for renewable-energy certificates and cost penalties for electricity producers which fail to surrender an adequate number of certificates.

127 "This was the conundrum in Copenhagen": Andrew Charlton, *Man-Made World*, Quarterly Essay 44, 2011, p. 5.

133 "This is classic Fabianism": The Fabian Society derives its name from the Roman general Quintus Fabius, known as Cuncator for his strategy of delaying his attacks on the invading Carthaginians until the right moment to strike. The first Fabian pamphlet in Britain carried the following note: "For the right moment you must wait, as Fabius did most patiently, when warring against Hannibal, though many censured his delays; but when the time comes you must strike hard, as Fabius did, or your waiting will be in vain, and fruitless."

WHAT FUTURE
FOR LABOR?

JIM CHALMERS

Election night on 7 September 2013 brought devastation for the federal parliamentary Labor Party and its supporters. It saw some very talented representatives defeated by a big national swing that put a full stop on the Rudd-Gillard era. For my part, it wasn't until well after 8 p.m. that I felt certain that I was the newly elected Member for Rankin, covering a large slab of Logan City and a handful of suburbs in Brisbane's south. Others, including the television networks, had called the seat much earlier. Cautious by nature, I had locked myself away with two colleagues in the small office of the massive former hardware store my team had commandeered for the campaign HQ, crunching numbers and taking calls. Outside, where the shelves of stock had once been, more than a hundred volunteers sipped on Fourex tinnies, ate spaghetti and watched the results roll in. Through tinted glass, I watched the room erupt when the ABC coverage noted an initial swing towards Labor in my seat, punctuating the gloom of the broader national political devastation that even the most optimistic Laborite knew was coming for us.

Earlier that day I drove through the electorate with my wife, Laura, through the suburb where I was born, another where I went to primary school, another where I spent most of my childhood and lived while studying at Griffith University, and yet another where I bought my first flat before moving down the street into the house we live in now. All within the current boundaries of Rankin and all in Logan City. Sustained by Laura's company, sausage-sizzle fare, four hours' sleep and adrenalin, we visited two-thirds of the forty-plus booths, meeting voters, shaking hands, thanking volunteers and fretting about the outcome. In the car between booths I composed in my mind a speech for the evening. As pessimism set in, I focused on words of concession. I had convinced myself that a wealthy opponent who had spent ten times what I had, and campaigned for twelve months longer, would be the first Liberal elected to represent the community I was born in, live in and love. A Sky News exit poll forecasting my defeat was quickly relayed by SMS to Liberal booth workers, who high-fived and, in one case, danced a little jig.

Few federal seats around Australia are homogenous, and Rankin is among the least so. What fed my pessimism on election night was a sense that while I had made specific connections with the diverse groups in my electorate, there was no overarching message that appealed to all parts of the electorate equally – a version of the problem we had nationally. In a cacophony of people and their aspirations, at home and around the country, we couldn't simultaneously satisfy diverse constituencies. My electorate, for example, has a core of lower-income families, pensioners and immigrants; a south-west of commuter suburbs dominated by utes and high-vis vests; an east comprising working families; and a north including wealthier suburbs just on the other side of the Logan–Brisbane border. There is a tremendous community spirit but little affinity between the areas when it came to voting. The gap was 30 per cent between my best and worst booths, perhaps among the widest in Australia, comparing 70 per cent in Woodridge with high-40s in Algester and Calamvale, and just 40 per cent in Daisy Hill.

The key to rebuilding the Labor Party after defeat is finding a new program to reunite our constituencies, without the luxury of the institutional advantages of a bygone era. The fragmentation of the old structures of working-class life, such as unions and the Catholic Church, upon which our organisational and electoral hopes once rested, has thrown up the representational challenges Mark Latham identifies in *Not Dead Yet*. There is hardly a challenge to Labor's future which isn't related in some way to his dichotomies – between aspirationalists and the underclass, and between inner-city progressive elites and outer-suburban cultural conservatives. Solving this constituent dilemma is the ALP's philosophical and electoral Rubik's cube. Getting all the colours to match up is our most daunting task.

Now that the political battleground is dominated by two extremes – the Greens and Tea Party wannabes – the task for this and following generations of Labor people is to fill the vacuum at the centre of Australian politics. That's why any useful analysis of the future of the Labor Party begins with this dilemma. To succeed electorally and philosophically we need to find new ways to unite the whole country behind a dynamic idea. This will be difficult, but not beyond us.

*

To understand the task ahead we first need to assess the Rudd-Gillard period. We need to understand the disconnect between Labor's stunning policy achievements from 2007 to 2013 and the decisive defeat we suffered at the election. The story of the past six years is one of policy progress and economic success untold and under-appreciated – partly because of division within the ALP caucus, to be sure, but also because of the poisonous politics practised by the "hyper-partisans" and the way this fed the deterioration of Labor's culture and relationships. Combined, these phenomena prevented Labor from sharing in the credit for Australia's achievements, particularly during the global financial crisis, and from uniting the country behind a plan for the future built on the pillars of Better Schools, DisabilityCare, emissions trading and the National Broadband Network. This created the essential preconditions for someone as extreme as Tony Abbott to slip through the doors of the Lodge, an awful prospect undreamt-of half a dozen years earlier.

These are some of the themes of the book I wrote early in 2013, *Glory Daze: How a World-Beating Nation Got So Down on Itself.* In it, I argue that the incentives in our political system are badly misaligned, which allows the hyper-partisans in the media and business to dominate the national debate in a way that pushes it to the extremes. This complex and costly combination of hyper-partisanship, short-termism, lobbying, rent-seeking, sloganeering, oppositionalism and circular self-criticism has poisoned Australia's confidence in itself and diminished Labor's achievements under Rudd, Gillard and Wayne Swan.

Despite the election result, the fight over Labor's legacy is not yet won or lost. The onus is on all Labor people, especially those who were part of the just-defeated government, to defend our policy legacy. It has been pleasing to see this recognised in the immediate aftermath of the 2013 election, even if couched in the negative as a way of avoiding the mistakes made after 1996 when the Hawke and Keating legacy was hidden in a cupboard far too long. Not one contemporary Labor figure has convincingly argued that it was Labor's lack of policy or economic achievements that cost it government.

There is a great deal to be proud of and salvage from the Rudd-Gillard era. Almost alone in the developed world we maintained an unemployment rate of under 6 per cent, and added almost 1 million jobs. Our economy is about 15 per cent bigger than when we took office, partly due to what Joseph Stiglitz described as "probably the best-designed stimulus package of any of the countries, advanced industrial countries, both in size and in design, timing and how it was spent." We bequeathed to our successors interest rates at record lows, inflation well contained, and debt a tiny fraction of our peers'. By any objective measure, economic management was the finest achievement of the Rudd and Gillard governments. Had we failed there, we would have been mired in the type of rolling crisis management we still see in comparable countries, and we would never have gotten around to key reforms like emissions trading, schools, disability services and much more.

As I argued in *Glory Daze*, economic reform has never been easy in Australia, but it is near-impossible in the current climate. One problem is the quickened pace and heightened partisanship of the media. Another is the straitened fiscal circumstances that make it impossible to soak the electorate with cash in a way that allows governments to buy reform without "losers." The third is the rent-seeking and hyper-partisanship that magnifies the opposition of a select few at the expense of policies designed to benefit the great mass of silent Australians going about their lives. This is the cost of Australia's lack of self-confidence: an unwillingness to change in ways that are difficult in the short term but deliver lasting gains to more people into the future.

Returning to opposition now begins a period of deep thinking and reflection for Labor. As we go about this, the best service we can provide the party is to maintain a focus on what kind of country we want, then to work backwards from that vision by colouring in the policies and structuring the party to best deliver bold national objectives. We must not get this the wrong way around: fighting over the institutional arrangements of a declining party, developing policies to satisfy different stakeholders, and then trying our best to stitch them together into an all-encompassing story, which is little more than an advertisement that does not survive a change of leader.

We did not make this mistake when it came to the big economic policy achievements and social reforms I have touched on. But Australians who did not discern a coherent narrative underlying this suite of policies can be forgiven their confusion. Whoever we blame for this, we can all agree that Abbott's election demonstrates that by the end of Labor's period in government our accomplishments were not matched by a widely shared sense of national achievement, unity or purpose.

*

Sometime during the 2012 American presidential campaign, Mitt Romney revealed himself as a fan of *Downton Abbey*. Within minutes the joke started circulating that of course he did, he thought it was a documentary. Tony Abbott is not quite a politically tin-eared plutocrat from central casting, but he is another self-confessed fan of *Downton Abbey*. And there, perhaps, hangs a political tale – that the nascent Abbott prime ministership represents something much more than a deficit of unity on the Labor side or any deficiencies in our 2013 campaign. It represents a smaller Australia, frozen in time.

The new prime minister's description of women "knocking on the door" of the cabinet paints the picture of a small group of middle-aged men taking decisions in a wood-panelled room behind lock and key – the cosy oligarchies of a bygone era returning to rule the roost: a nation robbed of the dynamism and creativity that comes from drawing on the broadest available talent, not just in politics but in the economy, dominated as it will be under Abbott by the well-funded noisy demands of the vested interests drowning out the disparate voices of working people, pensioners and small business.

Our country and our economy need to be *more* dynamic and *more* inclusive, not less. Labor's alternative vision for Australia should build on the conviction that the next economic success stories need not be selected from the limited, yellowing pages of the last. That there is not just room for more Australians to get ahead but that the future demands it. That dynamism and creativity come from harnessing the broadest possible workforce, one that taps women leaders, the work ethic of new migrant workers, the experience of seniors, the potential of disadvantaged communities, the technology for parents to work from home, the ingenuity and entrepreneurism of small-business creators, and the powerful imaginations of thinkers and innovators attracted to our shores by the promise of a more inclusive economy.

That's why Labor now needs to embrace the overarching theme of intergenerational mobility as the core organising principle of our policies. Intergenerational mobility is simply the idea that life choices and future economic contribution should not be determined at birth. Building mobility requires a focus on the tools of success – the means through which Australians can write their own destinies, provide for their loved ones, and get ahead. This can stake out crucial territory for Labor on the sensible centre and centre-left of the political spectrum. It will differentiate us from the backward-looking stasis of the conservatives under Abbott, and from the post-materialist obsessions of the Greens, which bear little resemblance to the hopes and dreams of middle Australia.

The idea of the "fair go" has been deeply ingrained in Labor values for more than a century. It is not only connected to Labor's past, but also to the country's future. Inequality has been on the rise for some time, and though research (by Andrew Leigh and others) shows no decrease in Australia's intergenerational mobility over time, the now-famous "Great Gatsby Curve" of the Canadian economist Miles Corak suggests that today's inequality will give rise to less intergenerational mobility in the future. Labor's mission in the coming years is to turn this around – to be more than the party of fairness and redistribution, but also of mobility and success.

There's nothing revolutionary in this, and even our political opponents will pay lip service to a lot of it. But there is a fundamental difference for Labor. At our core, we are Labor because we believe in economic mobility. These are words that trip off the tongue fairly easily, but when you stop and think carefully about them, you immediately notice two important things: one, no other political party in Australia actually believes in economic mobility; and two, it is an idea radically at odds with current social and economic trends.

Labor believes in economic mobility because we believe in the more contested political ideas and choices that underlie it – the ideas that the circumstances of your birth must not dictate your life chances, and that there is a role for the state in helping to create better life chances for the disadvantaged, both through enhancing their capabilities *and* through breaking open networks of privilege to admit people on merit.

The Greens obviously don't believe this because their animating policy concerns are post-materialist in nature. And the conservative parties more obviously don't believe in such economic mobility because they were invented to prevent it. Labor has held up half the Australian political sky since the election of the world's first labour government under Chris Watson. Conservatism has had to define itself in opposition to Labor for all of this time – to define itself in opposition to the aspirations of working people for a better life – first as protectionists and anti-socialists forming the Commonwealth Liberal Party in 1909, through Menzies' creation of the Liberal Party in the 1940s and the Coalition of today. That's the story as told by the history books, and it's no different today, be it in the unquestioning opposition of the conservatives to the mining tax or a billionaire starting his own party to look after his commercial interests.

Today there is a rising global trend of inequality, particularly across the developed world. The *Economist* reports that in the United States, for example, 95 per cent of the gains from the post-GFC recovery have so far gone to just 1 per cent of the population. Conservatives don't even bother to dispute the trend, preferring to argue that we shouldn't worry about it. Research connects this growing inequality to an even deeper concern about declining economic mobility. Corak's "Great Gatsby Curve," popularised by the chair of President Obama's Council of Economic Advisers, Alan Krueger, shows that the more unequal a society is, the more likely it is to have poor intergenerational mobility. In other words, inequality in one generation breeds further inequality in the next. There's a brutal logic to this, but one violently at odds with our national self-image, in which Australia is a place where anyone from any background can make a success of themselves.

*

Labor's focus in the coming term of opposition and beyond should be on creating the essential preconditions for genuine social and economic mobility, across suburbs and across generations. Having built and made sustainable the modern welfare state, and having deployed the tools of Keynesian demand-management to save Australia from recession, this is now the role for Labor in the modern economy. Having established better ways to redistribute wealth, we must now turn to better ways to redistribute opportunity. This means giving people the tools to be more successful participants in the market economy. It means promoting digital inclusion and a dramatic re-ordering of our budget priorities to create deeper, broader, more sophisticated pools of human capital and technological advance. Getting the policy right can deliver a virtuous cycle of political success, by creating a more inclusive base beyond public sector workers and declining blue-collar industries, reaching deep into knowledge industries, entrepreneurs and small business.

The idea of economic empowerment is not a new one. Taking from the work of the brilliant development economist Amartya Sen, Latham argues, "We need to think of inequality differently, as a threshold test" based on "the skills and capacity to benefit from economic growth, to be active in the community, to enjoy good health and wellbeing." And we need to "ensure all citizens reach an acceptable threshold, lifting up the disadvantaged so that, in acts of self-reliance, they can do more things for themselves." Sen's often-quoted dictum summarises the idea best: "poverty is the deprivation of opportunity."

A scan of the global centre-left and the ideas being generated by Labor's fraternal parties throws up some interesting ideas on how to colour in Sen's big picture. Take, for example, the concept of "predistribution" being developed by Ed Miliband in the United Kingdom. The term itself – described by the *Guardian*'s Martin O'Neill as "an unsnappy name for an inspiring idea" – comes from Yale's Jacob Hacker. To "make markets work for the middle class," Hacker advocates a "focus on market reforms that encourage a more equal distribution of economic power and rewards even before government collects taxes or pays out benefits." This means that "instead of equalising unfair market outcomes through tax-and-spend or tax-and-transfer, we instead engineer markets to create fairer outcomes from the beginning." It "is the idea that the state should try to prevent inequalities occurring in the first place rather than ameliorating inequalities through the tax and benefits system once they have occurred."

Much of the writing about predistribution centres on three kinds of policies. The first relies heavily on government regulation and direct intervention (for example, Miliband's proposed rail price caps). The second draws on a history of thought stretching back to the days of the mid-century political philosopher James Meade and, more recently, John Rawls, both of whom have advocated a form of "property-owning democracy." A third kind of predistributive policy has been described by Kitty Ussher as "the empowerment interpretation, which focuses on what is needed to ensure that an individual can respond to the uncertainties of a global economy in a positive and confident way."

The regulatory strain that sees national governments interfering substantially in the pricing of basic services may find superficial favour in a community burdened by cost-of-living pressures, but it is no way to foster a competitive economy. It is unacceptable for those of us on the centre-left wary of over-regulation and not yet ready to give up on the possibilities of markets. That's why the empowerment interpretation attracts us most. It is the best way to achieve our goal of broad, sustainable growth – by harnessing the capacity for people to get ahead, to be a confident and self-sustaining part of a dynamic and innovative economy.

According to Ussher, empowerment predistribution "is about striving to endow everyone – regardless of circumstances of birth – with sufficient weapons in their own personal armoury that they can achieve their ambitions and hopes even in the face of strong economic forces that seem daunting." It leads policy-makers down the path of heavy investment in human capital and the empowerment of workers so that, combined, they have the best chance of creating a high-wage, high-skill economy.

In this term of opposition, Labor's focus should be on policy development at the intersection of human capital and technology, recognising, as the *Economist* has, that "Many of the underlying causes of the growing gap between rich and poor – fast technological change and the rapid globalisation of the economy – are deep-seated and likely to persist." The magazine cites the view of Tyler Cowen of George Mason University that "the population will soon be divided into two groups: those who are good at working with intelligent machines, and those who can be replaced by them." The *Economist*'s recipe to address this is a "two-part agenda drawing on ideas from both left and right, aimed at reducing boondoggles for the affluent and increasing investment in the young."

An agenda based on heavy investment in young people is one that everybody interested in building intergenerational mobility should sign up to. It is the key to unlocking a more successful economy. That a traditionally right-wing, pro-market, pro-business magazine could point this way forward gives us a hint of the possibility of uniting business, workers and the community behind a dramatic reordering of budget priorities in Australia. In tight fiscal circumstances, investing more in human capital and technological capacity will require difficult choices. Given the future benefits to business, our first port of call should be business-tax concessions. We can strike a blow for economic mobility and tax simplicity at the same time by hypothecating money raised from closing tax concessions directly to investment in our economic capacity.

In time, Prime Minister Gillard's legacy will be regarded as a key part of the story of intergenerational mobility, especially when it comes to schools and disability services. By combining protections for workers with dramatic increases in investment in education and reforms to attack entrenched disadvantage, she has already followed the predistribution playbook. We can go further down this path, breaking new ground by reordering national spending to mirror the investment in human capital being undertaken by our competitors. We can do more to encourage students from disadvantaged backgrounds to enter our universities, with a combination of scholarships and mentoring. We can be more creative when it comes to digital inclusion. In this way, empowering workers need not be an alternative to market economics, but a way of allowing more people to succeed in a competitive, dynamic, growing economy.

*

On 13 September, as caucus members new and old filed into the Opposition caucus room, my mind wasn't on the loftiness of economic policy, Amartya Sen's work or the legacy of our just-defeated party. Only afterwards did I realise the cause of my melancholy: the last time I had stood in that room, beneath the portraits of leaders past, was on 4 December 2006. That was the day Kim Beazley was defeated by Kevin Rudd for the Labor leadership. It was also the day Beazley's brother had passed away. As the leader's deputy chief of staff, I had snuck into the back of the room to watch him deliver a classy farewell, full of emotion, praise for his colleagues and pride in the party. That speech marked the end of a more civil, loftier, thoughtful period in our politics, replaced with hyper-partisanship and poisonous politics.

The truth is that it wasn't necessarily Labor's policies or principles that saw us defeated in 2013, but fragmented constituencies and an internal culture tainted by the politics of polls and personality. The fact we were thrashed by a Liberal Party bereft of positive plans and unable to cost or properly explain its policies necessitates serious soul-searching. In the immediate aftermath of the election there has understandably been a focus on leadership. Understandable given the events of the last few years, but also because a defeat like that which we have just experienced cuts deep and people want to apportion blame. But the problem is broader than leadership; it is cultural as well.

Now each of us in the federal parliamentary Labor Party has a choice about how best to contribute to the broader discussion about future direction, learning from the past. As Sean Kelly, a former adviser to both Rudd and Gillard, wrote so convincingly, we need to cling to the best policy achievements of the last half-decade while discarding the worst internal obsessions.

Each of us might come up with different ideas. Some will focus on rules and structures, and they are very important. The democratisation push within the party has already made some impressive gains. But as one of my most astute campaign workers said to me on election night, the rules of the ALP are irrelevant if the culture is "stuffed." Culturally, we haven't gotten along sufficiently in recent years to press our policy advantage or superior vision. That's why the onus is now on all Labor MPs, and particularly on those like me, elected for the first time, to help repair caucus's culture in the new parliament. This means giving the "thinkers' faction" the intellectual freedom and encouragement to map the way forward.

For inspiration we should reflect on the words embossed on the simple print portrait of President Barack Obama, which hangs on the wall of my study at home: "Our destiny is not written *for* us, but *by* us." This is how I approach Australia's future and Labor's role in constructing it. We want a country where people have the capacity to be the master of their own destiny. Where, provided the tools to succeed, more people grasp the opportunities of a growing, vibrant, dynamic market economy fuelled by a growing, vibrant, dynamic population.

Genuine economic and social mobility requires a compact between government and citizen – and between generations – that government will maintain a decent social safety net and provide the requisite opportunities for more people to get ahead and provide for their loved ones. If we can unite the country behind an idea as simple as this, we can convince Australians that we are neither exclusively new or old Labor, not just the party of the poor or the successful, or of inner or outer suburbs, but a broad party for those who want to get ahead, writing for middle Australia a new chapter in our national story. A destiny written by people themselves, freed from the shackles of birthplace or ethnicity. A dynamic, wealth-creating market economy powered by that merit-based, more inclusive society.

The overwhelming feeling experienced by a newly elected MP is that a lot of people are now relying on you to stand up for them. Of course, the same is true of the Labor Party. We delivered for Australia over the last six years, yet the country still felt let down. The sooner we rebuild our culture, the more likely we are to come up with the necessary policies, ideas and vision to reunite the country and make amends.

JIM CHALMERS is the new federal Labor member for Rankin, to the south of Brisbane. Prior to his election he was the executive director of the Chifley Research Centre and, before that, chief of staff to the deputy prime minister and treasurer. He has a PhD in political science and international relations and a first-class honours degree in public policy. His book *Glory Daze* was published in July 2013 and he tweets as @JEChalmers.

ANDREW LEIGH

I was born in 1972, a few months before Gough Whitlam won office. When my mother's pregnancy reached the nine-month mark, she pinned an "It's Time" badge onto the part of her shirt that covered her belly. The Whitlam government lasted less than three years. Yet it transformed Australia's cultural outlook, foreign policies and social institutions.

Few commentators – regardless of their political stripes – would disagree with the notion that Labor governments do more. When Malcolm Fraser won office in 1975, he promised stability and moderation. When John Howard won office in 1996, he pledged that Australia would be "comfortable and relaxed." Tony Abbott has already sent out the same signals, vowing on election night to lead a government "which purposefully and steadfastly and methodically sets about delivering on our commitments to you, the Australian people."

There is a temptation – particularly after a heavy election loss – to judge governments by the number of years they stay in office. "You can't change the country from opposition," you'll hear the political hard-heads say. True as this is, it misses the fact that while being in power is a necessary condition for reform, it isn't a sufficient condition.

As Labor thinker Dennis Glover has noted elsewhere, longevity isn't the only marker of success. Vincent Van Gogh, Wolfgang Amadeus Mozart and Marilyn Monroe all gave more to their creative endeavours than a thousand pretenders. While each of them died before age forty, we remember them for the works they left, not the brevity of their stay on the planet.

I say this because Labor supporters must always remember that being in government means nothing of itself. Our pride must always be in what we have done while sitting on the right-hand side of the Speaker, not how long we manage to stay there. It's the policy achievements that count, not the years in office.

In the week before the election, I was reminded of this by 88-year-old Joyce of Ainslie, who wrote to thank the government for saving Australia from a repeat of the Depression she lived through as a young girl. And again on polling day at Lyneham Primary School, when a woman by the name of Deb asked her carer to bring her wheelchair over so she could say to me simply: "Thank you for DisabilityCare."

Over the past six years, Labor has many policy achievements of which we can be proud. On the international stage, we helped raise the prominence of the G20 and won Australia a seat on the United Nations Security Council. Our economy grew from the fifteenth-largest to the twelfth-largest in the world, productivity ticked up, and inflation and unemployment remained low by historical standards. On the environmental front, we trebled the marine park network to 3.1 million square kilometres, struck an agreement that allowed the Murray River to flow freely again, and put a price on carbon pollution that is already reducing electricity emissions.

If there was a policy fault with Labor, it was trying to do too much. Reducing problem gambling and pursing an ambitious federalist agenda through the Council of Australian Governments were worthy aims, but the outcomes we achieved did not justify the energy we devoted to them. Indeed, the 2013 election campaign might have been more effective if we had made fewer announcements.

Labor in government also spent too much time agonising about leadership. While it is probably the case that Australian campaigns have become more "presidential" over recent years, the change has been relatively modest (let's face it: most of the coverage of the 1961 election campaign focused "presidentially" on Robert Menzies and Arthur Calwell). Ultimately, federal politics is a team sport, with good reform requiring a strong cabinet. I find it hard to believe that the political trajectory of Australia would have been markedly different had Paul Keating replaced Bob Hawke a few years earlier, or if Peter Costello had successfully challenged John Howard. In opposition, Labor should concern itself primarily with working together as a cohesive unit. Teamwork, not a messiah, will take Labor out of the wilderness and back into government.

Labor must never forget that its brand is not interchangeable with that of the Coalition. Our two parties play fundamentally different roles in the Australian political system. Our role is to take the initiative, to defend those whom life has treated unfairly, to carve out an activist role on the global stage. By contrast, the Coalition parties are defenders of the status quo, more likely to be heard supporting vested interests than those on the margins of society, and largely untroubled if people turn off politics entirely. This means that Australian politics isn't Coke versus Pepsi, or even Hawthorn versus Fremantle. To become a Labor version of Mr Abbott's Opposition would be to repudiate the essence of what our party stands for. In government or in opposition, Labor must continue to be the party of ideas and reform.

In this essay, I lay out three possible futures for federal Labor: negativity, closed Australia or open Australia. From a political standpoint, each approach will be tempting, but I believe that only the third represents a sound path back into government. I then conclude with a discussion of what a philosophy of openness means for Labor's policy settings and political structures.

1. Negativity

Negativity is in some ways the most predictable strategy for Labor to follow. One lesson that will inevitably be drawn from recent Australian political history is that the way to win office is by denigrating the government, while minimising your policy differences with the party in power. The success of John Howard in 1996 and Tony Abbott in 2013 (and the failure of John Hewson in 1993) have reinforced the view that laying out all your plans for scrutiny is not the easy path to power. On education, the Coalition derided the Gonski proposals as "Conski," then flipped and supported our Better Schools plan. On debt, Mr Abbott assailed Labor's budget approach, then grudgingly committed to the same timetable back to surplus. On climate change, he went to the 2007 election supporting the scientific evidence and economic wisdom, denied both to win the Liberal leadership in 2009, and in 2013 says he supports the scientists but rejects the economists.

An oppositional approach has been made easier by the changes that have occurred in the media over recent years. In a speech on the economics of media reform in 2012, I argued that the 24/7 media cycle has the same effect on the political system as if we offered a cash prize for the parliamentarian who could come up with the most outrageous line of the day. A major driver of the shift towards shallowness is the rise of television and the decline of newspapers. In 1970, there were more daily newspapers bought each day than there were televisions in the country. Now, there are four televisions for every newspaper purchased. The changes afoot aren't ideologically neutral: they're particularly beneficial for populists and libertarians, and confronting for long-game reformers.

The negative approach echoes the strategy that federal Labor pursued in its first term of opposition after the 1996 loss. Amid disagreement over the extent to which Labor should embrace the Hawke-Keating economic reform agenda, the Labor Opposition focused on what it perceived as the shortcomings of the Howard government. From 1996 to 1998, it had plenty of raw material, with seven Howard ministers being forced to resign, a plethora of unpopular cuts, and the government's decision to seek a mandate for the GST at the 1998 election.

And yet it's not enough to outline what you're against. Plenty of Labor luminaries have made this point in recent times, so let me illustrate it with the words of the deputy Liberal leader Phillip Lynch, delivering the 1973 Deakin lecture:

> It is naively believed by some people that the one and only job of an Opposition is to oppose. This is a gross oversimplification. An Opposition's function is to compose as well as to oppose; it is a constructive as well as a destructive role. An Opposition is the alternative Government and, as such, must initiate and promote positive and constructive policies if it is to be regarded as a potential Government by the electorate. No electorate can be expected to endorse a political party which has become expert at criticism at the expense of its own initiative.

Opposition for its own sake has delivered short-term electoral success to Mr Abbott, but he will have difficulty translating it into a successful strategy for governing. Alfred Deakin's description of his opponents rings surprisingly true of the Abbott government a century on. In 1906, Deakin spoke of

> a party less easy to describe or define, because, as a rule it has no positive programme of its own, adopting instead an attitude of denial and negation. This mixed body, which may fairly be termed the party of anti-liberalism, justifies its existence, not by proposing its own solution of problems, but by politically blocking all

proposals of a progressive character, and putting the brakes on those it cannot block.

Negativity crowds out policy development. If your sole focus is on demonising the government, then the hard-heads will argue that putting forward your own ideas will only distract from the main task at hand. Yet we know from history that carrying out policy development in the full light of public scrutiny tends to make for better results. As former Hawke government adviser Bill Bowtell has pointed out, Medicare began operation eleven months after the 1983 election. This was only possible because the leadership spent the period 1977–83 consulting across the ALP and the health sector about the way that the policy would operate. By contrast, the most expensive policy Mr Abbott took to the 2013 election was paid parental leave, a plan developed by his own office with no process of open consultation across the Coalition, let alone the wider electorate.

Another consequence of negativity is to corrode the sense of hope, idealism and common purpose that is so vital to being a successful parliamentarian. After Tony Abbott took over as Liberal leader from Malcolm Turnbull in 2009, the incentives for backbenchers changed considerably. Under the Abbott Opposition, a backbencher who devised a fresh idea seemed to garner less respect than one who came up with a witty put-down of Julia Gillard or Kevin Rudd. Leaders shape their parties in many ways, but the rise of the backbencher-as-Rottweiler is clearly one impact that Mr Abbott has had on the Liberal Party.

2. *Closed Australia*

During the twelve decades since Labor's founding, our party has been wrong on immigration for longer than we have been right. Labor members were among the strongest advocates of the White Australia policy in the early 1900s. At the end of World War I, the Labor prime minister Billy Hughes resisted Japan's proposal to have a racial equality clause in the League of Nations Covenant. Ahead of the 1949 election, Arthur Calwell assured voters that "so long as the Labor party remains in power, there will be no watering down of the White Australia policy." It took Gough Whitlam's leadership of the ALP finally to put the party's worst racist tendencies to bed.

A similar story applies in the case of trade. At the time of federation, Labor members generally sided with the protectionists rather than the free traders. Labor supported the increase in tariffs during the inter-war era. And through the 1960s, Labor consented to the policy of "protection all round," through which quotas and tariffs combined to increase consumer prices and make firms uncompetitive. Again, it was the Whitlam government that began reducing protection, with its 25 per cent tariff cut in 1973.

Why worry about isolationism when the Whitlam, Hawke, Keating, Rudd and Gillard governments have all been internationalist in their outlook? The answer is that the pressures of economic nationalism are never far from the surface. While the 1996–98 electoral term saw federal Labor operate as a unified and effective opposition, it was also a period in which the party too readily distanced itself from the economic reforms pursued by Hawke and Keating. Indeed, Labor went to the 1998 election promising to abolish the Productivity Commission (the same body that would eventually help the Rudd and Gillard governments design DisabilityCare and reform the aged-care system). As Lindsay Tanner noted of this period, "Labor has continually offered support to disgruntled producer groups at the expense of consumers. Every time we do this, we take another small chunk out of our economic credibility."

Over recent years, the UK Labour Party has flirted with "Blue Labour," a more traditionalist, nationalist and populist conception of the party. I confess that Blue Labour's embrace of localism and history is appealing, but there are risks too. On trade, a "Blue Labor" ALP might be more open to protectionism and interventionist industry policy. On investment, it might be tempted to follow the agrarian socialists in the National Party by fearmongering about foreign investment in agriculture. On the environment, it might be more sceptical of market-based mechanisms. On immigration, it might seek to dramatically reduce inflows (British Blue Labour's Maurice Glasman suggested in 2011 a temporary freeze on all immigration except for a few highly skilled workers.). On foreign aid, it might follow the Coalition in abandoning any substantive commitment to raising aid to 0.5 per cent of national income.

Advocates of a closed Australia come in different flavours. Some oppose imports, migrants and foreign investment. But more commonly, people advocate raising the walls in just one or two domains. Some want higher tariffs but more migrants.

Others demand less foreign investment but support more aid. And there are those who believe we should have a smaller population but take more refugees. Whether the "closed Australia" model comes in part or as a whole, this is not a strategy that should tempt the ALP.

3. *Open Australia*

A better approach for the ALP is to embrace the record of openness that has been the hallmark of Labor at its best. Labor has always contained a social liberal strain – partly indebted to Chartist and Fabian traditions, but also influenced by social liberalism. In 1913, none other than V.I. Lenin sneeringly referred to the ALP as a "liberal Labor Party." The Australian philosopher Tim Soutphommasane argues that the social democracy of Anthony Crosland and H.C. Coombs owed more to liberalism than Marxism, summing up with the words, "We are all liberals now, comrade."

Throughout the twentieth century, social liberalism joined together many of Labor's achievements. Broad-based income taxation under John Curtin. A *Race Discrimination Act* under Gough Whitlam. Trade liberalisation and a floating dollar under Bob Hawke. Enterprise bargaining and native title under Paul Keating. An apology to the stolen generations and removing explicit discrimination against same-sex couples under Kevin Rudd. Carbon pricing and disability reform under Julia Gillard. Whether through support for individual liberties or belief in open markets, social liberalism has a prominent place in the story of the Australian Labor Party. In the excellent 2008 speech "Reclaiming Liberalism for the Left" and his provocative book *Hearts and Minds*, my colleague Chris Bowen also makes the case for liberalism.

This is an approach that is particularly appealing in light of the Liberal Party's steady abandonment of small-L liberalism. As George Brandis has noted: "Alfred Deakin, Robert Menzies, Harold Holt, John Gorton, Malcolm Fraser were all happy to describe themselves simply as liberals. Howard was the first who did not see himself, and was uncomfortable to be seen, purely in the liberal tradition." In 2010, Tony Abbott watered down liberalism further still, nominating three instincts that animate the Liberal Party: "liberal, conservative and patriotic."

What is occurring today is the undoing of the 1909 fusion between liberals and conservatives. Small-L liberals like George Brandis and Malcolm Turnbull are distinctly in the minority. It is little surprise that genuine liberals like Malcolm Fraser and John Hewson spend more time criticising than praising the party they once led. As the political commentator Peter van Onselen argued in 2012, "It is high time the Liberal Party changed its name to the Conservative Party." To adapt a US quip, theirs is a LINO Party – Liberal In Name Only.

Labor will always be the party of egalitarianism. Too much inequality can tear the social fabric, threatening to cleave us one from another. A belief in equality is deeply rooted in Australian values, and underpins policies such as progressive income taxation, means-tested social spending and a focus on the truly disadvantaged. This marks Labor apart from many in the Coalition, who maintain that inequality does not matter, that economic outcomes have more to do with effort than luck, and that government can do little to reduce poverty.

In also taking on the mantle of social liberalism, Labor states our commitment to open markets as the most effective way of generating wealth. This isn't a theological belief; it's a practical one, grounded in centuries of human experience. Where markets improve wellbeing, we should use them. Where they don't, we shouldn't. To borrow a phrase from the Harvard philosopher Michael Sandel, ours is a commitment to a market economy, not a market society.

In the realm of social policy, liberalism is the belief that tax cuts are preferable to middle-class welfare. It also requires more of what Franklin D. Roosevelt called "bold, persistent experimentation." Australian policy could do with a few more randomised evaluations, the better to sort out what works from what merely sounds good.

Many of Australia's greatest successes in fields such as farming, science, sport and medicine have been grounded in practical experimentation and rigorous evaluation. There's something very Australian about being willing to try new things, honestly admit failure and learn from our mistakes. We need more of this in politics. Good policy evaluation isn't just a better feedback loop, it's fundamentally about a more modest approach to politics. As the US judge Learned Hand once noted, "The spirit of liberty is the spirit which is not too sure that it is right."

Social liberalism also means an approach to politics which is at least as concerned about the nation's low entrepreneurship rates as the decline of manufacturing. One which ensures that anti-dumping laws increase competition, not reduce it. And a politics that acknowledges the power of market-based mechanisms to address environmental challenges: from water buybacks in the Murray-Darling basin to a price on carbon pollution. Good economic policy should also involve being open to more creative uses of income-contingent loans to manage risk, such as for drought assistance or sports scholarships.

A commitment to social liberalism would also pledge Labor to an open and multicultural Australia. Multiculturalism, as Soutphommasane argues, draws on both liberalism and egalitarianism. It recognises that all citizens have equal rights, but also that different cultures are valued. Listening to the first speeches of Labor members, I sometimes wonder what our party's founders would have made of the paeans to multiculturalism and migration that are common to almost all Labor maiden speeches in recent years. Many of Labor's founders regarded Asia's peoples as the biggest threat to their living standards. By contrast, social liberalism recognises that Australia benefits from immigration (including circular migration). It also acknowledges that national growth isn't like the Olympic medal tally: prosperity in China, India and Indonesia will boost Australian living standards too. To borrow the title of Lindsay Tanner's 1999 book, Labor should support an "Open Australia."

What openness means for party structures
Until this point, I have focused on the policy directions that Labor should follow in the coming years. But the approach

of openness also has implications for the party's organisational structures. In selecting candidates, we should aim to follow a process that is as democratic as possible. Where party membership is strong, this means a ballot of rank-and-file members. Where membership has dwindled, we should move to a plebiscite of the electorate, conducted by the Australian Electoral Commission. Similar rules should govern the selection of Labor's Senate candidates in all states and territories. We should also allow ALP members to directly elect important party positions, such as delegates to the national conference and members of the national executive. The Queenslander William Kidston, the world's first Labor treasurer, summed up our creed as: "The ballot is the thing." Labor members have been staunch supporters of the secret ballot, universal suffrage and – more recently – an Australian republic. In this spirit, Labor should never flinch from making our party structures more democratic. It will help ensure that we attract a broad diversity of representatives, and use our selection processes to build community support for our candidates.

At the same time, openness demands that we keep some space for non-factional members. (Since I'm one of only a few non-factional members in the federal caucus, you're entitled to say, "He would say that, wouldn't he?" – but please, hear me out.) Factional groups have always existed in the ALP as in other political parties. Party members should always be free to join them. But the freedom to join a faction should sit alongside the freedom not to join one. It is vital that all levels of the ALP manage to find a way to accommodate Labor Party members who opt to remain independent. One reason that factionalism has increased over recent years is that many important positions are allocated by votes at party conferences rather than by ballots of the membership. I would guess that at least one-third, and maybe over one-half, of Labor Party branch members are not in a faction. But at most state, territory and national ALP conferences, the share of non-factional delegates falls to less than one-tenth. This means that independents are under-represented on everything from state policy committees to the ALP national executive. Allowing party members to have a say directly is not only more democratic, it also helps to create some space for independent members of the ALP. Indeed, given how personally painful it can be to people to switch factions, even the factions themselves might benefit from structures that don't force ambitious new members into joining a faction immediately. If ALP members are able to make their way outside the factional system, then those who do join a faction will probably make a more considered decision about which group to enter.

Naturally, this has implications for the power of unions in the ALP. Ours is a party formed out of the union movement, but that doesn't mean that the relationship between our industrial and political wings needs to remain as it was a century ago. For example, some have proposed removing the requirement for ALP members to join a trade union. More radically, others have argued for engaging union members directly in the party, rather than through their leadership (in much the same way as British Labour are now seeking to do).

In either case, the ALP should tread cautiously before changing our relationship with the union movement. We should also be alive to the way in which other changes to our rules have an indirect impact on the relative power of unions within the ALP.

A policy of openness could also involve providing more flexibility to Labor parliamentarians on how we vote in parliament. At present, a Labor representative who crosses the floor faces expulsion except if the issue is a so-called conscience vote. In practice, issues of "conscience" are really those with religious overtones: they include RU486 but not Afghanistan, same-sex marriage but not the Northern Territory Intervention. I find much to like in Chris Bowen's suggestion that the ALP should adopt the British Labour policy of a "three-line whip," a system in which the message sent out about an impending parliamentary vote is underlined one, two or three times. One line means members can vote as they please; two lines means that members are expected to vote one way but face no sanctions if they cross the floor; and three lines means the vote will be enforced. This contrasts with the present system, in which one-line votes only exist on "conscience" matters, and two-line votes do not exist at all.

Adopting a more flexible caucus voting system would acknowledge that the main differences within the Labor Party caucus are not based on religion (which is what the current conscience votes reflect). As it happens, it would also change one of the features of the Labor Party that led Alfred Deakin to fuse his liberals with the Australian conservatives in 1909. Deakin liked much of what he saw in

Labor representatives, but could not abide the strict party discipline of the ALP. While it may have been right for that era, I believe that Labor would be better served by a more flexible "whipping system" today.

Openness may be the right road for Labor, but it is not the easy one. After losing government to what Anthony Albanese has tagged "the Noalition," it will be painful for Labor in opposition to adopt a more positive approach. Perhaps some of our supporters will argue that the real reason Labor lost the 2013 election was that we did not embrace economic nationalism across the board. But if Labor is to serve its core mission – of raising living standards, spreading opportunity and encouraging diversity – then we should pursue openness in our policy settings and our party structures.

ANDREW LEIGH is the federal member for Fraser. His latest book is *Battlers and Billionaires: The Story of Inequality in Australia* (2013).

TROY BRAMSTON

Nine days after Gough Whitlam became leader of the Labor Party in 1967, the party's former leader, Arthur Calwell, addressed a trade union dinner in Sydney. "Those who wish to weaken the influence of the trade unions are enemies of the party and the trade union movement alike," he bellowed. "The Labor Party was founded by trade unions and nobody else. It has always been based on the trade union movement. It can never rest on any other foundation and still be the Labor Party." Sitting in the audience with a look of utter contempt on his face was the man who had replaced him as leader. Whitlam, however, was unfazed. He had filed an article for the next day's the *Australian* titled "Labor and the future." On the question of trade unions, Whitlam was clear. Labor's future as a party of the centre left with links to unions was not in doubt. But Labor's future role within the parliamentary system was at stake. "Our actions," he wrote, "in the next few years must determine whether [the party] continues to survive as a truly effective parliamentary force capable of governing and actually governing." Whitlam had fired the starting gun for the reform crusade that he would unleash as leader in the coming weeks. His mission was to dilute the power of the party's faction and union bosses, open up decision-making and rebuild the party's links with the community. He envisaged a Labor Party that was based not just on unions but also on the broad mass of people who represented modern Australia. More than four decades later, Labor is again at the same reform crossroads.

There are many people now calling for systemic reform to the Labor Party. Mark Latham has made a welcome contribution to this debate in *Not Dead Yet*. John Faulkner and Darcy Byrne from the Left of the party, and Chris Bowen and Sam Dastyari from the Right, are also important reform advocates. But they are almost entirely silent on one vital area of reform: the party–union nexus. Latham acknowledges the roots of "union power" in the party, its corrupting influence on policy and its corrosive impact on party culture. And he correctly identifies how this power is obtained and administered: "Union power is now exercised through centralised control: union secretaries donating money and staff to marginal seats and rounding up the numbers at state and federal Labor conferences," he writes. But Latham, like most leading reform advocates, does not offer any proposals for reform because he believes they will never succeed. As Latham told me when he was writing *Not Dead Yet*, "I'm applying a discipline of looking for practical, feasible solutions." This is understandable. But this pragmatic approach has hemmed in one of the more astute observers among a class of Labor men and women who generally lack intellectual curiosity or a capacity to "dream the big dreams," as Paul Keating used to say. The holy grail of reform is to revisit the party's relationship with the trade union movement. Nothing is more fundamental to rebuilding the party's community links, renovating its policies or reforming its culture.

The recent Independent Commission against Corruption hearings into the former NSW Labor government provided a window into the party–union relationship. The allegations of corruption, and the subsequent findings of corruption regarding the NSW Labor Right sub-faction boss Eddie Obeid, have been well aired. ICAC also examined the activities of the NSW Labor Left, which nurtured and supported the allegedly corrupt former minister Ian Macdonald. In February 2006, when the then NSW Labor assistant secretary Luke Foley told union bosses over a Chinese meal that he wanted to remove the faction's support for Macdonald to remain in the NSW upper house, he was overruled. Two powerful Left-aligned unions, the Construction, Forestry, Mining and Energy Union and the Australian Manufacturing Workers' Union, would not wear it. Macdonald was endorsed for another term in the upper house, despite Foley's concerns. This is how power is exercised in the Labor Party.

To truly understand where this power comes from, it is necessary to examine the party's structural relationship with trade unions. Trade unions select 50 per cent of the delegates to the party's state conferences. Delegate numbers are allotted to a union based on that union's number of members. The delegation's composition is determined by the union secretary. At the conference, these delegates sit together and vote as one, as directed by the union secretary. This enables a union secretary to bargain with other powerbrokers to win their hoard of votes. Conferences determine policy, elect party officials and decide Senate and state upper house pre-selections. Unions regard spots on the party's executive bodies as "theirs" to fill. They expect to have "their" delegates to the party's national conference elected by state conferences. They demand seats in parliament for "their" candidates. And they get them. This power is also exercised informally. Joel Fitzgibbon, the convenor of the NSW Labor Right faction in Canberra, told me in December 2012 that "trade union blocs" are able "to control individual MPs." Anybody in a position of power who challenges this – an MP, a party official, a conference delegate – will soon find their own position under threat. A faction, or faction boss, has power only because of the votes they control at party conferences. This is why reducing the proportion of union delegates at conferences is critical. Without a reduction from 50 per cent to perhaps 20 per cent, no reform will ever fundamentally transform who exercises power and how they exercise it throughout the party. More broadly, the influence of unions in the party is pervasive. Most members of Labor's frontbench during the Rudd and Gillard governments have either worked as a union representative or as a lawyer for unions. Unions send their staff to marginal seats to work to elect Labor candidates. They pump money and other resources into local, state and national campaigns. As Labor's most successful leader and the union movement's greatest advocate, Bob Hawke, said, unions today exercise "an almost suffocating influence" on the party. It is untenable.

The hollowing-out of the party's membership – down from 150,000 members in the 1930s to 50,000 members in the 1990s, to 44,000 today – has been coupled with a rise in the influence of unions. As members have been squeezed out from participating in the party's key councils or standing as candidates for parliament, the influence of a political class dominated by unions and political staffers has grown inexorably. Concomitantly, as Latham recognises, the party in government has become vulnerable to policies that prop up old smokestack industries, re-regulate the labour market, denigrate skilled migration and propagate class warfare. The great party–union partnership for reform in the 1980s and 1990s has dissipated. As Bill Kelty argues, unions today lack leaders who are prepared to advocate trade-offs in return for economic reforms that are in the national interest. For Labor in government from 2007 to 2013, the party–union relationship became an albatross around its neck rather than an electorally beneficial relationship of constructive engagement in the national interest.

Simon Crean, like Hawke, led the industrial and political wings of the labour movement. In the last week of the 2013 election campaign, I spent two hours with him in Melbourne talking about his life in politics and the union movement. After serving as secretary of the Storemen and Packers Union, Crean was elected ACTU president in 1985, two years after Hawke became prime minister. "The most exciting time in all my public life was being at the centre of the Accord period," he said. "It changed the country for the better. We lent credibility to a Labor government in terms of economic management because we delivered on where we had previously struggled. For the first time, we showed what the labour movement could do for the nation when it shared the economic agenda." It is a lesson worth learning from Labor's past as the party today settles into what is, at the very least, likely to be two terms in opposition. Working in the national interest, not just self-interest, is a lesson that stems not only from the Hawke-Keating governments, but from earlier periods of Labor history too. Recently, the Australian Workers' Union republished *History of the AWU*, about the formation of the union, written by its co-founder William Guthrie Spence. Labor historian and speechwriter Graham Freudenberg writes in an introduction to the book that when the unions and the party have been able to find "the spirit of common purpose, compromise and common sense," the party has succeeded in government.

Union influence has increasingly encroached into the parliamentary party. Whitlam, Hawke and Keating were never beholden to unions to support their leadership. Kevin Rudd was, in part, undone by unions who witnessed first-hand his instinctive distrust of union powerbrokers. When he returned to the prime ministership, he did so without the support of any of the major affiliated trade unions or many of their delegates in parliament. In contrast, Julia Gillard's leadership was actively supported by union leaders. These leaders did not resile from their right to state publicly that Gillard should lead the party or organise support for her. In return, Gillard encouraged, even courted, an expansion of union power inside the government and the party. At the February 2013 AWU national conference, Gillard aligned her government, and the party, to the union cause. "I'm the leader of the party called the Labor Party deliberately because that is what we come from," Gillard said. She rejected the moderate, progressive and social democratic labels that Whitlam, Hawke and Keating happily embraced. Gillard led a union party. "That is what we believe in and that is who we are," she said. It was an extraordinary speech. No modern leader had previously spoken in this way about the party–union relationship. No modern leader saw their party in such narrow terms or appealed to such a diminishing audience. Early Labor leaders actively set out to broaden the party's philosophy and platform so that it appealed to a wide range of voters, regardless of class and regardless of whether or not they held a union ticket. In the modern era, no Labor leader since Calwell has been more beholden to, or more of an advocate for, union power.

The party was formed by the trade union movement in 1891. Born of the collective struggle for workers' rights, Labor has a sentimental link with unions as well as a structural one. The union link informs the character and culture of the party. In 1986, the outgoing NSW premier, Neville Wran, warned the party not to break its links with organised labour. Wran remains the party's most popular leader and its greatest election winner in the modern era. He supports the union link but believes, like Hawke, that the unions wield too much power. In 2011, then aged eighty-four, he told me in an interview that Labor had "lost its way," as its candidates no longer represented the community. He said Labor too often failed to field candidates with life experiences that reflected those in the wider community. "We've developed the political career path," he said. "On our side, it is university, union, ministerial or MP's office and then stand for an election. This path keeps the new practitioners away from the reality of life of those they hope to represent. If you've been in that cloistered world, how can you expect to know what the real world is like, what issues the real people face and the aims and aspirations of those real people?" He surveyed the newly elected Liberal MPs after Barry O'Farrell's crushing 2011 electoral victory in New South Wales and thought many belonged in the Labor Party. "Those people are now conservative representatives and we have to get them back as Labor representatives."

Labor does not need to sever its links with unions, but it does need to reinvent them. Partly, it is about modernising the structure of the party to reflect the community. According to a recent ACTU research paper, "Urgency & Opportunity," union membership is not keeping pace with workforce growth. In 2011, there were 1.8 million members in a workforce of almost 10 million, a decline of 31 per cent since 1990. Over the same period, employees increased by 34 per cent. Union density was 40.5 per cent in 1990; it is now 18.4 per cent. In the private sector, it has fallen from 31 per cent to 13 per cent. In the public sector, it has declined from 67 per cent to 43 per cent. In short, the unions are losing the membership battle. The industries with the most members are in the government sector: education and training (39 per cent); administration and safety (36 per cent); electricity, gas, water and waste services (32 per cent); and transport, postal and warehousing (32 per cent). They are struggling in the private sector where industries are experiencing the strongest employment growth. So if unions no longer represent one-fifth of the workforce, how can they represent one-half of delegates to Labor conferences?

It may not always be in the unions' best interest to be so linked to the Labor Party. Indeed, many unions are not affiliated to the party. They, like all unions, have their own voice. During the 2013 election campaign, I sat down with ACTU secretary Dave Oliver and ACTU president Ged Kearney. We met at the ACTU's campaign headquarters located inside the 125-year-old Trades Hall on the edge of Sydney's Chinatown. The unions played a critical role in the campaign in marginal seats. Their efforts may have helped to save several Labor seats in New South Wales and Queensland from falling to the conservative parties. But this campaign architecture had to be rebuilt for 2013, because the $30 million Your Rights at Work Campaign, which helped Labor win power in 2007, had not been maintained or built on. "We spent years building the movement into a campaigning movement and then overnight, with the election of a Labor government, we went from being a campaigning organisation to a transactional organisation," Oliver said. "We thought a lot of issues could be resolved by going to Canberra and negotiating our way through things."

So, in July 2012, Oliver and Kearney persuaded affiliated unions to amass a $12-million campaign war chest by imposing a $2 levy on its two million members over three years. The aim: to rebuild its campaigning capacity. In about nine months, the ACTU developed the most sophisticated voter-targeting strategy outside the major political parties. Its purpose was to turn undecided voters who are union members into voters allied to the unions' cause on polling day. For the first time, the ACTU persuaded its affiliated unions to share their membership databases so voters could be targeted in key seats. They started with 415,000 union members in forty-one seats. They found there were more union members, on average, in Coalition-held marginal seats than Labor-held marginal seats. Each union member was contacted and asked a series of questions about the issues that motivated them, their past voting record, who they were likely to vote for and if they could be persuaded to support Labor. As the electoral battleground changed, so did the strategy. In the final weeks of the campaign, the ACTU and its key unions targeted 125,000 voters in thirty-three seats who could decide the election. Their efforts were critical in helping Labor to stem seat losses.

The unions campaigned on issues that were relevant to their members. But they also played an important role in supporting the Labor Party, which was also in their members' interests. This is the sort of role unions can continue to play in the community by expanding the voice of their members and campaigning on issues that matter to them. But the party–union nexus must also modernise and adapt. It must not be about powerbroker politics where union bosses wager the support of their union to advance the careers of politicians, elevate or tear down party leaders or barter for favourable policy outcomes. It must be, as Whitlam said, about giving working people a voice inside the Labor Party and working towards common objectives that are in the national interest, rather than simply serving each other's interests.

In July 2013, a special meeting of the Labor caucus held at the Balmain Town Hall – just a short walk from where the party was founded in 1891 – adopted the most significant reform in its history: the direct election of the parliamentary leader by a college of MPs and party members, each with equal weighting. It is a reform that many (including me) had long advocated. But nobody really believed this would happen so soon. Rudd Redux changed that. There is a case for the franchise to be broadened to include a component that includes union members. This is similar to the British Labour Party's leadership electoral college. The reform will be debated at the party's next national conference, due in 2014. This would allow perhaps 1 million members of unions affiliated to the party to have a say in electing Labor's parliamentary leader. It would leave the newly elected leader open to criticism that they are a simply a union candidate. But in reality, a union secretary could not easily marshal the votes of so many members. Rules could also be put in place that prohibit actively campaigning for a candidate or corralling votes. This would further transform the leadership election contest into a large-scale exercise in popular democracy, chosen by people who share the values of the Labor Party. It is worth debating.

In several states the party has experimented with primary-style pre-selection contests, where party members and members of the public vote to select Labor's candidates for office. Another idea worth exploring is giving union members from affiliated unions a say in pre-selections. This was recommended by the party's 2010 *National Review* report, which suggested union members comprise 30 per cent of a pre-selection college vote. The party should revisit the Australian Labor Advisory Council model, where union and parliamentary party leaders meet regularly. It was largely abandoned during the Rudd-Gillard years. When the party was formed in 1891, individual unions affiliated to local party branches. This encouraged union members to have a say inside the Labor Party on local matters. This should also be considered. Labor's archaic branch structure has long been a challenge for party reformers. The party should relax the branch rules and allow dedicated workplace branches to be established where unions could play a key role.

Labor must also embrace a suite of other reforms to its philosophy, policies and culture. I addressed these in my 2011 book, *Looking for the Light on the Hill: Modern Labor's Challenges*. In that book, I argued that the party is suffering an identity crisis. Labor is unclear about what it stands for and what its values are. Senior figures struggle to communicate the party's broader goals and to persuade the public of the merits of its policy ideas. The party's core objective, the socialist objective (the very animating purpose of Labor in politics) has remained largely unchanged since 1921, but it does not adequately describe Labor's governing traditions or provide inspiration for the party's future. Labor's identity crisis, a challenge for many centre-left parties around the world, was exacerbated by the experience of the Rudd-Gillard government. Labor in government did not live up to its own lofty aspirations. Promises were broken. Policies were abandoned and then rebirthed. The party lacked a compelling narrative that crystalised its vision. The Gillard government was seen as beholden to the Greens or independents, riddled with factions, tarnished by backbench scandal and its policy development driven by focus groups and polls. The disunity that plagued the government seemed only to amplify the perception that the government lacked a driving purpose other than being riven with personal rivalries and competing ambitions.

Labor must now learn from its defeat. Labor's primary vote is the lowest since 1934. This is a truly dismal result. Barely one in three voters chose Labor. The party's greatest election winner, Hawke, said it best on election night: "This is a very major defeat." Labor is not without achievement during the past six years. The party will cherish the apology to the stolen generations, the response to the global financial crisis, the National Broadband Network, DisabilityCare and the Gonski reforms to education – albeit, still to be delivered. There were also many policy failures and political misjudgments. The most significant reason why Labor failed to turn around its fortunes in the past three years, in addition to the difficulty of running a minority government, was the bitter internecine war between Rudd and Gillard. Crean identified this as the tragedy of the Rudd-Gillard years. "Their strength was in their combination," he told me. "And that strength showed up most of all in the first three years. The tragedy was the fracturing of it, from which we've never recovered."

But it would be a mistake for Labor to believe that disunity was the *only* reason for its defeat. The day before the election, Labor's pollster, UMR, sent a report to the party's hierarchy with the results of its final round of polling in key marginal seats and a separate analysis of why voters had deserted Labor. The UMR report showed the key reasons for voters switching to other parties was in-fighting and disunity followed by its policies on asylum seekers, the impact of the carbon tax on electricity prices and concerns over economic management, the budget deficit and debt. Disunity was the chief reason for the government's defeat. But the equally important take-out is that it was the failure to develop, implement and articulate effective policies that led millions to turn to other parties. Voters also named the lack of policy consistency and clarity as a concern. Again, this is the identity crisis that, in addition to organisational reform, must be Labor's focus in the next few years.

After the party's greatest crises – Jim Scullin's defeat in 1931, the debacle of Arthur Calwell's leadership in the 1960s or the Whitlam dismissal in 1975 – Labor's great strength was its ability to renew and reform itself for a new era. Labor already has a blueprint for reform: the 2010 *National Review* report written by party elders Steve Bracks, Bob Carr and John Faulkner. The report said the party was facing a "crisis of membership." The tragedy for Labor is that Gillard scuttled the report. First, she refused to release two-thirds of the report dealing with Labor's time in government and the 2010 election campaign. Second, she failed to throw her weight behind the reforms at the party's 2011 national conference. It was a terribly disappointing moment for the party's true believers. Party reform has succeeded only when the leader champions it. This was the experience with Whitlam in the 1960s, Bill Hayden in the 1970s and Crean in the 2000s. Gillard was not a reformer when the party she led needed it most. Of the thirty-one recommendations put to the conference from just one-third of the report, only thirteen were fully adopted – fewer than half.

A few weeks after Whitlam became Labor leader, he addressed a Labour Day dinner in Melbourne. His speech was the polar opposite to Calwell's banquet oratory a few weeks earlier. Whitlam argued that trade union participation in the party "must not merely be rhetorical, but real and representative of the whole trade union movement." Entrenching the power of union bosses, who propped up Calwell's leadership (as they did Gillard's leadership), was not what he had in mind. Whitlam wanted Labor to once more be a mass party that represented the diversity of the community. Labor should consider how to encourage the 1 million affiliated union members – everyday men and women from a variety of trades and professions – to play a role inside the party, rather than be ruled by around 100 key union apparatchiks. As I have outlined, grassroots trade-union members could play a role in selecting local candidates, joining local party branches, participating in policy development and perhaps helping directly to elect the party leader. But the critical structural link between unions and the party, cemented at state conferences with a 50 per cent bloc vote, should be reduced to around 20 per cent. Unless the party is prepared to slash the proportion of trade union delegates at party conferences, the vice-like grip that union and faction bosses have on the party will not be broken.

Troy Bramston is a columnist with the *Australian*. He is the author of *Looking for the Light on the Hill: Modern Labor's Challenges* and editor of *For the True Believers: Great Labor Speeches That Shaped History* and, most recently, *The Whitlam Legacy* (2013).

LOUISE TARRANT

Australia is one of the most affluent nations on earth, as Mark Latham goes to such lengths to point out. And, consequently, in Latham's view, collectivism is dead. As he sees it, today's workers have prospered to the extent that they have outgrown unions and each other. They are self-reliant, have limited expectations of the state and are uninterested in politics.

Latham blithely ignores the impact of the profound restructuring of the Australian economy, and hence Australian society, over the past three decades or so. Instead, he vilifies unions and blames them squarely for the Labor Party's woes. He simplistically tars all unions with a "corrupt and self-serving" brush, eroding the very legitimacy of workers' ability to act collectively. Such vitriol coming from a former Labor leader landed, as was no doubt intended, like a body blow, and must have given great delight to Australia's outspoken political right as it echoed their own remonstrations.

But Latham has done us a service by belling the cat of plenty. Unpicking his argument, we can better understand why so many workers feel that Labor has lost its way and why formal politics seems so removed from people's experiences. This is the key question Labor Party reform must address.

Australia's key political conundrum is this. In the face of protracted economic growth and consequent long-term gains in household income, how is it that "rising cost-of-living pressures" can be so effectively and relentlessly hammered for political gain? Indeed, the flavour of parliamentary debate in the months leading up to the September 2013 election would suggest Australians are living in precarious circumstances. Hence we heard from the Liberal MP Craig Kelly that the rising cost of living is "driving a dagger into the heart of middle class working Australians." Much of the cost-of-living alarm was predictably voiced by Coalition MPs in their pre-election jostle to position themselves against Labor. However, it fell on fertile ground, including many electorates once regarded as Labor strongholds.

If the Labor Party is now to rebuild in the face of its 2013 electoral failure – and to refashion progressive politics for the twenty-first century – it is this contradiction that must be understood and addressed. Any number of economic studies and statistics can be used to make the same broad case Latham puts forward – that is, "We've never had it so good." But at the same time many Australians genuinely feel they are both disenfranchised and struggling. Why is this so?

Any snapshot of modern Australia will tell you that we are earning more. Over the past two to three decades a significant amount of wealth has been generated within the Australian economy. As the NATSEM *Income and Wealth Report 2012* concluded, growth in Australian household income has steadily outstripped price rises over the past twenty-seven years. A 20 per cent increase in our disposable incomes in real terms over that period means the average family is now effectively $224 better off per week. We might argue about the relative weightings of inputs like housing in NATSEM's calculations, but it is true that this rising tide has lifted all boats.

This might suggest that the great Australian working class, on which the union movement and Labor Party were built, has moved on. According to Latham's new world order, mass organised labour has given way to fragmented work-forces, a new generation of aspirational small-business own-ers has left Labor behind and throngs of mobile, flexible individual workers are following the jobs. With all those working families building McMansions in suburbia, who needs Labor? Yet this is far too simplistic a take on the com-plex shift in the fracture-lines of power, politics and money that has remade contemporary Australian society. And as such, it risks overlooking the new divisions to which progres-sive politics must respond.

The new great Australian divide

From where I sit, Australian society is certainly not divided into the buoyant, aspirational ranks of the employed "haves" and a welfare-dependent underclass of unemployed "have-nots" that Latham suggests. There is another important group emerging among working Australians. Some Australians do continue to enjoy job security and once-standard conditions of employment such as sick leave, holiday pay, overtime and weekend penalties, as well as legal protections such as health and safety regulations and workers' compensation. However, an ever-growing number of working Australians are entering the ranks of the long-term insecure.

Today, one in five Australians is a casual employee – from cleaners to academics – and one in six Australians relies on the minimum wage. In many cases these groups overlap, creating new, acute pressures on workers and their families when insecurity and low pay collide.

This trend represents two profound shifts in our society, with deeply felt consequences for individuals and their families. For Renna, a United Voice member from country New South Wales, it means real constraints on the family budget: "I don't think my family should have to sweat, freeze or live in darkness because we can't afford power." And for Allan, struggling to pay bills and meet his family's needs: "I have to work 45-plus hours a week to pay the bills, and all I want is more time with my family."

While power has steadily shifted from workers to business owners, risk has been steadily shifted away from business owners and back onto the shoulders of workers. The notion that labour can be purchased like any other input – and its supply increased or decreased depending on the prevailing business climate – means, nowadays, that business risk can be effectively laid at workers' feet.

Meanwhile, governments have steadily sold off the family silver, privatising public utilities and services, pushing private health insurance and other "user-pays" models that constantly load more costs into the family budget. Members like Monica from South Australia understand only too well the impact of a reduced safety net: "I was a single parent myself so I know how hard it is. Juggling work, if you can find it, and young children is a real challenge. Single parents need more support, not the big cuts to benefits that the government has made."

For richer and poorer – declining equality in Australia

Against this background, the NATSEM data on wealth generation can be read in a more accurate light. Many lowly paid and even many moderately paid workers are, in fact, under considerable financial stress, while much of the rest of our society also feels under considerable financial pressure.

A close look at consumption patterns and household costs reveals that while incomes have been rising, so too has the proportion of fixed household costs that those incomes must cover. A 2006 US analysis by Elizabeth Warren, for example, found that

> in spite of the growth of dual-income households, and contrary to the mantra of luxury-driven excess, [increase in] household consumption was, in fact, driven by a rising proportion of fixed expenses (housing, child care, education, health care, transport etc.) – rising from around 54 per cent of household income in the 1970s to 75 per cent in 2004."

A 2010 report by the University of Sydney's Workplace Research Centre, commissioned by the ACTU, found similar consumption patterns in Australia. So while income has risen, so too has the resort to credit, loans and ever larger mortgages to finance both the costs of modern living and make up for the new economic risks imposed by less secure employment.

The net result is this paradox of plenty: many workers – almost regardless of their income levels – feel burdened by the stress of working hours that are too short or too long, insecurity and greater levels of debt. That so many people feel they are constantly stalked by financial burdens is no surprise; in the mid-1980s household debt sat at around 40 per cent of income, today it's closer to 150 per cent.

The consequence of this gradual shift in power and risk is a less equal Australia. The rise of an affluent Australia from the end of the Depression in the 1920s to the 1980s was characterised by increases in both wealth *and* equity. The increase in wealth since 1980 has been marked by an increase in wealth across the board, but considerably larger gains at the top. The top quintile of Australian income earners have gained 70 per cent in their standard of living since 1988, making them the equivalent of $32,000 a year better off, while the bottom quintile have gained 42 per cent, making them $4300 a year better off. This trend is, in fact, reversing some of the equality gains of last century. As Andrew Leigh noted in his book *Battlers and Billionaires*, the income share of total earnings commanded by the top 1 per cent fell from 12 per cent in 1910 to 8 in the 1950s and 5 in the 1980s. By 2010 it was back up to 9 per cent and climbing.

The biggest driver in household debt levels is the cost of purchasing or renting a home. Any number of statistics can be trotted out to make this case. Australian average house prices increased 147 per cent over the past ten years, for example, compared to a 57 per cent increase in household incomes. In 1991 the median house price was five times the average income; by 2011 it was seven times the average. The average first-home loan had risen from three times the average annual income in 1996 to six times by 2010. The list goes on. Not surprisingly, the Australian Bureau of Statistics records that in 2012 only 31 per cent of Australians owned their homes outright, down from 42 per cent in 1994.

For renters, who are often the lowest income earners, shut out of the housing market, stresses have become even more acute. In the last five years rents in capital cities rose twice as fast as inflation. For United Voice member Andrea, renting is the big challenge: "The rent takes half my wages every week, so it is really hard to survive." Andrea's is not an isolated case, with 44 per cent of lower-income earners who rent officially living in "housing stress" – that is, spending more than 30 per cent of their household income on housing costs.

Catherine from Queensland speaks for many United Voice members when she says: "If I were prime minister, I think making housing affordable would be the first thing on my agenda." Curiously, although 84 per cent of Australians rated housing affordability as more important than education, border security and broadband access in the lead-up to the 2013 election, the election campaign barely reflected these deep concerns.

In one thing, Latham is right. Neither Labor nor the unions can afford to hark back to the past; massive structural changes have taken place and more change is to come. But far from putting itself out of business, Labor remains both relevant and critically important to Australia's future, far more so than its recent electoral showing would suggest. As a large grassroots union in close touch with hundreds of thousands of Australia's lowest paid workers, we have recently reset our direction. We believe this experience, and the insights it offers, has broader significance for the Labor Party, the union movement and, perhaps most importantly, for the values that underpin a fair Australian society.

Who is United Voice?

According to Latham, Australia's working class "has gone the way of record players and typewriters – a social relic irrelevant to the future shape of the Labor movement." United Voice members would be surprised to hear that. We are workers who look after your elderly relatives and educate your young children; we offer you a smile with your drink at the bar, wait on tables and keep our hotels and motels ticking over twenty-four hours a day. At night we fan out across the city. We are the anonymous cleaners who maintain your offices, schools, shopping centres and public toilets, and the security officers who keep watch – among many other roles.

Until a couple of years ago United Voice was known, in the great Australian tradition of contractions, as the "Missos," from our former name the Liquor, Hospitality and Miscellaneous Union. It was an appropriate term, really, given the diversity of our membership coverage. We made a decision to change our name in 2011. In doing so we removed the "union" tag. That wasn't because we wanted to disassociate ourselves from the union movement and its collective representation of workers. Rather, it was because we wanted to broaden our role to reach beyond traditional, narrowly focused workplace bargaining.

Kim, a United Voice leader and casino worker from Tasmania, best captures the sentiment with her description that "Our union is stepping out of the workplace." In addition to doing the critical work of representing our members' interests at work, we wanted to take on the bigger issues that affect members and their communities, those so-called working families our politicians talk endlessly about. Hence, United Voice.

One of the first things we did was to redirect our efforts back to the grassroots. Under the banner of "Real Voices for Change" we started thousands upon thousands of conversations with our members. To make these conversations meaningful and valuable we set out with a big question: what is it that makes a good life? Detailed responses from 26,000 members have produced unprecedented personal insights into what it means to be working class in Australia today. It's easy enough to make encouraging noises about engaging with the grassroots. In reality, it's a long, hard, detailed job that never ends. This conversation must continue if it's to become the basis on which a union, or a progressive political party, works.

Reforming Labor

United Voice is the second-biggest union affiliate on the floor of the ALP's national conference. The future of the Labor Party really matters to us and our members. Equally, it could be said that we have a lot of institutional power at risk in any reform process. But having power in an organisation that fails to represent our members properly, which is incapable of winning voters' trust and provides no real impetus for workers' engagement, is an empty reality. In fact, if there is one thing our members and Mark Latham would agree on, it is that there is something fundamentally broken with the Labor Party.

We believe reform is necessary. We believe the Labor Party needs to be more accessible and that the branch structure needs to change. There needs to be a greater role for rank-and-file members, but it must be genuine. Currently the majority of the rank-and-file national conference positions are held by current or former politicians and their staff. If additional rank-and-file positions are to be created they need to be real. Accountability lies at the heart of much of our members' angst with the party and the performance of its parliamentarians. We believe therefore that all candidates should face pre-selection and all existing parliamentarians – senators included – should face re-endorsement. The Labor leader should be elected by members and caucus, but members, like caucus, should have a recall power. We also firmly believe that affiliation with unions should remain a defining hallmark of Labor, and that unions need to create new possibilities for their members to engage in party activities and leadership.

One example is the post-election Labor leadership ballot, an important opportunity to break from a purely factional response. We emailed or texted almost every one of our

120,000 members asking them to nominate issues that matter to them and invited the candidates to respond. All members were then asked to vote on who they thought should be the Labor leader. This is, of course, largely a symbolic gesture; our members do not have a collective vote through their union in this ballot. But it is part of breaking away from the old mould and learning new ways of engaging members in a new type of politics.

However, the party-reform debate cannot simply focus on structures and electoral systems. Resolving what Labor stands for, and whom Labor stands with, needs to be the primary focus.

Losing touch with working people

Many of our members despaired during the recent election, listening day in and day out to politicians failing to speak to their concerns. They heard plenty about public deficits but little about private debt or high interest rates on credit cards or crippling mortgage repayments. They heard lots about policy costings, but little about policies that will help them with their own costs – how to beat rental hikes, pay off home loans before retiring, access bulk-billing doctors or tackle utility price blowouts. Instead they were subjected to the unedifying spectacle of Labor and Liberal politicians fighting over "me too," and offering indistinguishable political visions that failed to speak to, inspire or motivate working people.

One United Voice leader and disability worker, Wanita, was spot-on when she called to account politicians in general and Labor in particular: "Unless we can change politicians, there will be no hope. They're not listening to people. They don't understand the issues."

In addition, many workers expressed real anger at the ill-discipline, internal disunity and the self-indulgence of Labor's parliamentarians while in government. Many working Australians see formal politics as failing them, particularly the party that should be their champion.

This is not just a devastating potential epitaph for the Australian Labor Party, but a diagnosis that bodes poorly for democracy itself in this country. People committed to a fair, just and sustainable future know that any withdrawal of the citizenry's passion for, and engagement with, politics leaves a vacuum which money and privilege will readily fill.

Understanding contemporary unions

Part of the responsibility for workers' loss of faith in politics needs to be shouldered by unions themselves. Unions too often institutionalise politics, creating an aloof mystique about how it operates and failing to engage members sufficiently in political activity. Unions should not be exempt from any review of the Labor Party's malaise or its future agenda.

But I do shudder every time I hear "a comrade" use neo-liberal arguments to marginalise and demonise workers and their unions. One of the most pernicious aspects of the Latham-Hawker-Cavalier ALP reform contributions is their characterisation of and attack on unions. Such undermining means workers' very rights to organise, bargain and act industrially and politically are now under attack from *both* sides of politics. These are the same rights that have underpinned Labor since its inception and that are fundamental to progressive politics. Such criticism demands a response.

Firstly, unions in Australia have always been driven by a broader ambition than simply advancing their own members' interests – hence the focus on raising minimum wages and standards across the workforce, campaigning for social wage advancements and securing legislative protections for future generations. The legitimacy and efficacy of this activity is not necessarily contingent on raw membership numbers. It was assumed, and until recently accepted, that unions represent working people, and therefore act in their interests.

But clearly that representative function is under extreme challenge despite the majority of Australian workers being covered by either awards or enterprise agreements. There is no denying that union membership has declined, but so too has an environment that facilitated workers organising. Gone are the closed shops, the preference clauses and the centralised wage fixing of the 1970s. In the 1970s, the attacks on unions were about their exercise of power. Today's attacks are about the very existence of union power.

As such, it is very important to differentiate between raw number, or "size," and the notion of the "right to represent." The Queensland Labor Opposition is small in number, but this doesn't negate its right to represent the values and interests of Labor people. So entering into a debate about whether the union position within the ALP should be 50 per cent or some other number misses the point about unions' broader representative role. Unions represent working people and work for that broader objective. Today, employer-generated resistance – both in their attitudes and how they structure their workforces – makes it much tougher going than it was in the past, but this does not render this critical role illegitimate.

Second, the legitimacy of union officials to act as representatives of their immediate union members has also come under fire in the Labor reform debate. I have no problem with valid criticism of individuals or particular practices. However, to claim unilaterally that union officials act entirely in their own interests and without regard to their members simply undermines workers' ability to combine and express their collective interests through their elected union representatives. Consistent with the principle of representative democracy, union officials participate in party structures as elected and accountable representatives of their memberships – giving voice to members' concerns and aspirations just as they do when negotiating with an employer, representing members in legal proceedings or lobbying governments. It is not unreasonable to advocate for greater participatory democracy both in unions and the Labor Party, but simply to dismiss the legitimacy of representative structures is to weaken workers' voices.

Third, Latham's view of unions is entirely out of date. Radical change within modern unions has been underway for some time. Today, Australia is one of the most hostile environments in the developed world for workers to organise and collectively bargain. Ask any North American or European union and they are amazed that, given our entirely open shop laws, the decentralised and limited scope of our bargaining system, the highly deregulated labour force and the employer's capacity to effectively obstruct bargaining and lock out workers, we have survived at all. Adapting hasn't been easy and I'd be the first to say we have more progress to make. But don't write us off so easily – or gleefully.

Indeed the Carr-Bracks-Faulkner review pointed the ALP in the direction of the union movement to learn how to reorient itself in a changing world with particular reference to learning from unions' innovative growth and campaigning strategies and capacities. In the case of United Voice, the number of workers joining our union every year is the same as the total size of the Labor Party. Our biggest growth in recent years has come from small disparate workplaces in the service sector, from diverse nationalities and cultures in cleaning, and from young women predominantly in early-childhood education and care.

Latham is simply wrong when he asserts that "grassroots union activism in Australia has ended." Clearly he has never encountered our amazing cleaning members engaging the big end of town or our indefatigable early-childhood educators canvassing parents, shoppers or politicians. If he had, he couldn't be anything but moved by these members' vibrancy, their commitment to collective endeavour through their union and their leadership of these campaigns. They are the union.

Every time someone from "our side of the fence" condemns unions, they put a little lead in these members' saddle.

Fourth, Latham uses the Health Services Union scandal to condemn the entire union movement. It is cheap point-scoring. No one condones misuse of members' money, and bad or illegal practices should be criticised and stamped out when they occur. But in United Voice there is a clear understanding across all officials, staff and committees of management of the significant financial and emotional commitment our members make to being a member of United Voice. Our code of conduct is unequivocal when it states,

> It is the highest honour and privilege to be an elected representative of United Voice members. Every action of every representative of our union carries the hopes and aspirations of hundreds of thousands of members – past, present and future. The highest level of integrity is expected, the highest level of dedication assumed.

These are not just words but cultural and organisational commitments consciously fostered.

Again, creating suspicion, inferring wrongdoing and reinforcing notions of union illegitimacy simply aid those who wish to undermine workers' capacity to organise for an effective voice in their workplace and the community.

The challenge for progressive politics: what next?

One of the big unresolved dilemmas for social democratic parties worldwide is their place in a neoliberal world. The ALP in the 1980s embraced aspects of this agenda, tempered some of its excesses and tried to harness the gains and redistribute them as fairly as they could. But this raised many questions – not least around historical notions of the state, the market and civil society. These tensions remain largely unresolved. Just witness the brutal battles around privatisation in Queensland, New South Wales and Western Australia.

As a result, it is far more difficult today to articulate what the Labor Party stands for. Just as neoliberalism has sought to normalise itself through shifting and redefining community values – from the communal to the individual and from citizen to consumer and investor – this too has challenged historically held Labor values. The 2009 party platform identified core values such as social justice, compassion and a fair go. By 2011 the "enduring values" were cited as opportunity, responsibility and fairness – words more often than not spruiked by the right. It is a live question: does the ALP today have a foundation of agreed values? The answer goes to the heart of the party's appeal, its contract with working people and its commitment to progressive politics.

This is the first stage of any party reform process – to debate and decide the values of a 21st-century Labor Party. We need to renegotiate what social democracy looks like. We need a vibrant party, inclusive and active. And we need to build a strengthened labour movement – unions and party – working in tandem, mutually reinforcing, creating the vision and capacity to transform the future. It's daunting but doable. It is the determination of Cathy, a cleaner and United Voice leader from South Australia, that should guide us when we think about the future: "It's on a path to be worse … It's our challenge to make it different."

Louise Tarrant is the national secretary of United Voice.

GUY RUNDLE

When the author of *Not Dead Yet* rose to prominence in Australian politics in the 2000s, it appeared that there would be two prominent Lathams in Australian political history, Mark joining Sir John Latham who, in the 1920s, came as close as anyone to dismantling the centralised wage-fixing at the heart of the Australian settlement. In more recent years I've come to conclude that there are two Lathams within Mark Latham himself. One is someone determined to think deeply about what the good life would be in modernity, what we should aim for, and how to reconstruct a progressive politics to achieve it. This is the Latham who began his *Diaries* somewhat bluff and bumptious about the dynamic and positive powers of the market, and ended them, one scarifying election later, driving through Sydney's western suburbs, disturbed by the appearance of the fortress-like McMansions, families walled in from each other, living off cable television rather than communal life, and Latham sounding for all the world like the judgmental leftists he had hitherto criticised, Adorno in a Monaro. He understood something then, about what happens to a society with privatised prosperity, and the dilemmas it creates for a mass progressive party.

There is some of that in *Not Dead Yet*, but there is also the other Latham, the somewhat simplistic marketophile, advocating policies based on thin evidence that purport to be based on non-ideological problem-solving, but are really the projection of a pretty fixed idea of human life and Australian society – and this limits the usefulness of the essay for the reconstruction of Labor as a progressive party.

Indeed there were times reading it when I recalled the story of Bernard Shaw meeting Sam Goldwyn, when the former undertook a lucrative screenwriting deal. Goldwyn rabbited on about theatre and ideas, only to be interrupted by Shaw remarking, "The trouble with you, Mr Goldwyn, is that you want to make art; I want to make money." As someone from the left that Latham defines himself against, I want the ALP to be a viable mass political party, capable of winning elections and advancing a steady and realistic progressive platform, giving people the opportunity for better lives. I thought Latham's essay would be in that spirit, and a corrective to Clive Hamilton's Quarterly Essay 21, *What's Left?*, which wanted the ALP to be a crusading left social-democratic party on a macro level, well out of kilter with the way average Australians think about their lives. Latham presents his marketophile policies as if in answer to a popular demand, when they ought rather be presented as a personal preference.

Latham correctly identifies a core problem for Labor, the decomposition of its class base into sub-classes with divergent interests. Hitherto, the unemployed were simply the usually employed currently without a job (even when, during the Depression, that was 25 per cent of them).

Now, prosperous trades and service/care workers have income and assets dividing them utterly from the minimum-waged, dividing those in turn from ongoing welfare recipients. Policies that once simultaneously tackled inequality and improved the mass of people's lives are now split; what addresses inequality often disadvantages the high-waged with extra costs. Tackling inequality among various sub-classes must either be done by appealing to a universal interest and obligation – just as society is becoming steadily more atomised – or be "smuggled in" under cover of policies addressed to a prosperous majority. Since it is the majority policies by which the ALP lives or dies electorally, I'll focus on those.

Latham's argument, as I understand it, is that Labor should reaffirm its successes in creating a market-driven economy by attacking various myths – such as a cost-of-living squeeze – head-on, and should then advance a social policy for aspirationals, with education and opportunity expansion at its core. His suggested mantra for this reorientation is, "What would Keating do?"

Well, maybe. But I have to admit that some of this is more reminiscent of late Keating – the Keating of, "What are people going on about?" and of kissing the ground at Kokoda to try to change the way Australians understood their history. The dual problem here is that if you're going to attack a widely held myth with statistics, you better make sure there's no reality to the myth. And you better not mistake your own myths, such as "aspirationalism," for an unquestionable reality.

Most people want better lives, for themselves and their children and those close to them – but the idea of "aspirationalism" is a very particular and rigid rendering of it. As Latham constructs it, it has a relentless quality, a ceaseless advancement to it, expressed in accumulation and grim Tiger Mother–style education for the kids.

That social vision is advanced by most of the current ALP elite past and present, whatever their other differences. Of course it is. They're all driven people, members of a lifelong political caste, and they project that assumption onto the general electorate as the only way to live your life. There seems to be no understanding that most people don't live that way; that's why they're most people, the average, by definition. The idea of a better life encompasses many incommensurable things – not merely better houses and material things, but more free time, more family time, ease of life, security and a certain centredness in their own existence. Past Labor leaders understood this, and so did John Howard – he took it over by telling people they should be able to feel more "comfortable and relaxed." That wasn't just about Keating's perceived advancement of a cultural liberal agenda; it was about the sense Labor had established in the early 1990s that everyone was on a forced march from the suburban "Settlement" society established over a century to … God knows where. Bob Hawke had kept a lid on such enthusiasm, won four elections (and is almost unmentioned in Latham's chronicle of leaders); Keating ramrodded it and lost the farm. In the ensuing years, elements of the NSW Right have developed an enthusiasm for the market that amounts to a repudiation of the mixed society/economy that made this country one of the best places to live a working/middle-class life in the twentieth century.

This vision leads to some flat-out absurdities: "Five years later [after the 2008 crash] history's verdict is still clear: open, free markets work better than any leftist alternative." No, they don't. The most successful societies are the north European social democracies, enterprising but secure, poverty all but abolished, inequality – class, gender, race – relentlessly attacked. IKEA, H&M, Volvo – three global brands from a semi-socialist society. Name three Australian equivalents. Elsewhere, Latham argues that no technical innovation has come from the state, which is sheer embarrassing ignorance: try the computer, antibiotics, the jet, the agricultural green revolution, the internet and the web, for a start.

Such marketophilia is clearly delusional, and so too is the notion that things will be improved by equating "aspiration" with the desired good life. Combining the two in an education policy creates an evidence-free policy prescription for social betterment. In noting the models of educational success, Latham mentions Finland – but only in passing and on the way to some grim Asian-style vision of relentless work, parental cooption and ruthless competition. No wonder: because in creating the best education system for a European-based culture, Finland has eschewed everything Latham suggests. Schools have shorter hours, later starts in life, no performance assessment for teachers, conditions that the Australian Education Union could not hope for even at its most militant, and a lack of parental involvement. Why isn't this canvassed as a possible model? Because it is recognisably leftish, I suspect. Latham's education prescriptions, which have a slightly crankish specificity, are in service to his idea of how he would like the culture to be, rather than how it is. Most importantly, it is contradictory at its core. He wants a market-driven culture that maximises individual autonomy – and then to penalise financially parents who don't help with their kids' homework. Yeah, that's a vote-winner. Thank God we've abandoned statist paternalism.

This is presented as a prescription for Labor, but it's really a restatement of its current failure. This is what people really, really hate about the ALP at the moment: the simultaneous insistence on an ever more testing market economy from the right, and a left that has decided to identify itself with micro-managing behaviour, à la plain cigarette packaging. What makes it even more comical is that its grandees walk around telling each other how they've got their finger on the pulse of the electorate. As with Michael Costa, Cassandra Wilkinson and other marketophiles in higher places, it is difficult not to feel that the ancient enemy is, as always, the ALP Left, and that that epic struggle dictates a politics which is then presented to the Australian public as "what they want."

This is all a pity, really, because the other Latham recognises the central dilemma for a rational, progressive party: that it must respond to people's desires for more individually expansive lives even as it prepares for the civilisational challenge of climate change effects. The answer for such a party is surely to listen to what people want, and focus on the things that joint the present to the future. Leaving aside old left–right battles, that is surely about addressing what people are complaining about when they talk of cost-of-living pressures. Australians are squeezed in a wider sense: ludicrous house prices, poorly designed cities, overpriced (private) services, free-time poverty etc. Surely what bridges us to a climate change society are policies that open up real choices in people's lives – affordable, good housing, more flexible work, support for social caring roles, child care and better parental leave options, multi-life-stage higher education – offered not as coercive impositions, but as real alternatives to a parallel high-consumption lifestyle. Modest, targeted, realistic policies that centre on the ALP's support base and don't get distracted by what cannot be regained (the IT crowd, whom Latham hymns as aspirational, vote Greens at a rate significantly higher than the general public; Latham and others better get used to the idea that the Greens will grow as the information class grows, and this change will eventually deliver them an inner-city Lower House base). From the left, I'm suggesting a politics conformed to where the Australian public is. So sometimes is Latham, and one would like to see more of him. Sadly, *Not Dead Yet* was mostly written by the other Latham, the engineer/brand-manager of human souls, pushing markets and Mem Fox readings on a public that want something more.

*

Terry Eagleton, in a review of forgotten nineteenth-century utopian novels, picked out one for special mention. In it, the society of the future had become so perfect that "in church, the best pews could no longer be reserved by the fine families." In other words, the capacity to imagine how things might be otherwise was so limited that many people in everyday life – and these utopians were as everyday as any –

could not see the changes that would make their lives better. The only thing that could change how they saw the world was change in the world. Constrained by a world of work, church and duty, they could not imagine how first the eight-hour day, then half-Saturday, and finally the achievement of the weekend, would change the whole basis of social life. Suddenly people (men, mostly, at first) could breathe in the time between work and sleep; could become themselves, pursue their own interests and passions – and thus a different way of life came into being. The civic institutions – the parks, museums, libraries, sports clubs – created to serve that new free time expanded the notion of equality contained within it. To own a painting is one thing; but there is no way that someone can look at a painting in a public gallery better, richer, than another person. The left/social democratic/labour movement, by reshaping political and economic conditions, brought a new way of life, a new way of being human, into being. But it was not simply a different way of being human – it was a more human way of being human, and everyone can recognise it as such, once it is achieved. In the decades before the 1910s and '20s and the achievement of things like the "weekend," block vacations etc., it was difficult for many people even to imagine these. The basic setting was that life was more or less a continuous chain of work – and it was in some ways easier to conceive of an overthrow of the system entirely than it was to imagine a different rhythm of life. The idea of two whole labour-free days – really, only finally nailed down in the late 1940s and early '50s – was a different sort of thing. Now, imagine what you could take away from the Australian public before they actually rose up and occupied the streets. Quite a lot, I suspect, but touch the weekend and you would have an instant and bona-fide uprising on your hands.

Such a history of social change – one could cite dozens of examples – could be put alongside Latham's idea of "light-touch social democracy." There have been too many huge policies and institutional revolutions, he complains, and too much social policy is leftist social engineering. And in any case, all the important social reforms have been done. A Whitlamesque lifelong welfare system is now in place. Gough and the rest of us can rest easy. History ceased when the NDIS was laid down and Sam Dastyari began to reorganise the NSW Right.

The tangle is perfect. The overly paternalistic social policy that Latham advances in the educational sphere – Singapore (further) down under – is exactly of the type that he ascribes to the left.

By contrast, the end-of-history social democratic state he describes is in reality a half-built social-market state, in which people are trained to lower their expectations until they meet the services available. Latham appears to be lowering his with them.

This is simply the "weekend" effect writ large in social policy. Take health policy as an example. For a century, health-care reform has come up against the notion that the latest reform is it, that we got there. When free public hospitals were introduced, some hardy souls suggested that it would be good if everyone had access to a GP, which was howled down. When the UK National Health Service was started and that was achieved, it was muttered that perhaps people could see a specialist before a health emergency, but this was declared flatly impossible. When this became viable, nutrition, rehabilitation and mental-health services came to the fore. These are not simply incremental changes. They are reimaginings of health as a service; and whatever private component of them might exist, such reconstructions can be done only as a public enterprise (if one is to avoid a ghastly inhuman US-style system).

So let's stop drawing a line and imagining we have reached the end of history, and go from the other end – a realistic, genuinely social democratic system. That for me would involve a system in which unnecessary tragedy, in medical terms, had been reduced to its smallest possible size. By this I mean no tumour missed because the local health centre didn't have a mini-MRI, no heart attack passed over because the local hospital doesn't have a 24/7 consultant cardio, no diabetic without a quarterly endocrinologist, a mental-health system which was never without a bed for an acutely psychotic person, and so on. That would be combined with the core promise of the NBN – to mitigate the geographical disadvantage regarding surgical expertise – and other techniques to *transform what health care is*. Sooner or later the sheer technological advance makes it first desirable, then essential, to wholly reconstruct the way health is done. Thus, eventually, the hospital/health centre/clinic trinity could be reconstructed. Do we need these behemoth hospitals as the core health facility in an era when once-rare equipment like ECGs is now standard? Were one to upgrade community health centres to a new type of institution – a sort of Health Focus, capable of most of the existing functions of the hospital, rather than merely a few of them – would we change healthfulness and risk categorically for the better? Would that not change social processes such as sick leave, for example? With a Health Focus close by, sick leave could be more divisible, measured in half-days and hours, thus making it less likely that people would defer essential preventative appointments. When you factor in the increased possibility of home-working, job-sharing, the NDIS and its futures, it becomes clear that the health insurance system would need substantial reorganisation and rethinking. The aim of all this would be to make the stories we still tell each other today – "The GP missed the tumour, otherwise she would have made it"; "He felt odd, but there was a two-hour wait in casualty so they never got the minor heart attack" – to be as distant and vanished as the "He went out in the rain, got pneumonia and died" or "She couldn't afford the pills and died" tales of pre-antibiotic, pre-NHS health care.

To do that, to beat back the most residual diseases to their minimum occurrence, is what the left/progressive movement does. Our aim is to minimise avoidable tragedy, to make unnecessary suffering small enough to drown in a bathtub. Would anyone to whom this scheme was presented say it was a leftist agenda? Or would they say instead that it is a universal agenda, one that only the most austere classical liberals and libertarians would gainsay, and that the role of a progressive party is to present to their potential supporters the *particular* political, social and institutional forms that will fulfil their *general* desires about the form of life they would like to have.

So that is the horizon. If we work back from it towards the present, we can then deal with all the proper objections: we cannot yet afford it; the public–private mix of delivery should not be set in stone; we live in a society with a low tolerance for high taxes. But what is crucial is that we start at the horizon and move back to the present, and thus orient ourselves to being on the midpoint (at most) of the journey. For if we do not, we end up in the Latham trap. Schopenhauer remarked that most men mistake the limits of their thought for the limits of the world. In presuming that we have reached an endpoint in the development of progressive social institutions, Latham mistakes the limits of the NSW health system for the limits of the world.

Moreover, it's not only in social and state institutions and systems that Latham imposes limits that – had they been imposed by earlier generations of progressives – would have left us with a more limited, less human society. Latham argues that people are increasingly self-steering individuals making their own path through life – as opposed, I presume, to an earlier mass society, subject to mass institutions and collective processes. That's a one-dimensional reading by any measure. Is it so certain that today's aspirationals are more self-determining than the working-class couple of the early '50s who lived well on one wage, grew some of their own food, repaired their own objects, read the pamphlets of the NCC or the ALP or the Communist Party (which in the early '50s, could sell 80,000–100,000 copies a pop) and found their entertainment in neighbourhood, church, union etc. groups rather than in enormous amounts of mass-produced media? They were certainly more immune to the propaganda of privately owned media, as pernicious then as now – more capable of reading it for the sports, and ignoring the rest, because they had a living alternative political tradition to draw off. Today our choices are manifold, but they come in a series of sealed boxes. The people in the McMansions that Latham sped past at the end of the *Diaries* – are they more or less self-reliant and self-determining than the earlier generation? Yes, they have vastly more choice in education and jobs, mobility etc. But many of those jobs are pseudo-differentiated and highly patterned, new suburbs are as cookie-cutter – and more so – than the ones developed in the post-war era, contact with non-friendship groups is minimal and atomised, and consumption of mass-produced media occupies a much larger part of life. Not discounting the many new and welcome pleasures of such a life, does that really leave greater space for self-determination – or does it instead create a culture in which media has a *greater* power to form mass opinion, based on exclusion of information and propaganda, than it once did?

Fully opening out that question would take a book in itself, but we need only to concede that this is possible to suggest that a progressive party has a large role to play in campaigning for real and categorical choices in life, and to create a critical sense of what is and isn't changeable in social life. Latham appears to see a very happy populace, content with their lot. I don't doubt that many people say they are happy and feel the whole shape of their life to be acceptable – mainly because I've seen people say that in the deep south of the US, when they're living on part-time work from Walmart, off tinned food at the Bide-a-Wee motel, with no health care. Likewise, you would get the same sort of answer in 1907, from the workers who benefited from the "frugal comfort" of the Harvester judgment. Indeed, for many years, the ALP was a workerist party, rather than a genuinely social democratic one, suspicious of benefits not tied to wages. It is only when such parties reconceive their role in relation to the class they represent that they gain the possibility of standing back from the social processes within which they work. Genuine social democracy orients itself to the idea that the full ensemble of human needs and desires – for security, opportunity for flourishing, for love, work and play, and for meaning – should be the benchmark against which current social arrangements are set. By that measure, it is quite possible to say that people will genuinely attest to their happiness – but that things could be better. Crucially, it is to say that things could be better in a manner that can only be achieved by collective and statist action on a grand scale. People will always work towards accepting something of their present circumstances – that's how they maintain an equilibrium. But when you question people on the specifics of their lives, rather than the generalities, you find a different story.

As I noted in the first part of this essay, most urban Australians are subject to a "squeeze," whereby luxuries have become cheap, while necessities – say, home ownership in decent proximity to work – have become onerous. Since the

Hawke-Keating period, Labor has largely acquiesced to the idea that vast swathes of everyday life should be run by the market, with only the worst affected helped out of penury. Decade after decade, an acceptance has bedded down – that home ownership demands two full salaries, going full-tilt, that child care should be only partially subsidised, that commuting should eat up two to three hours of the day, that urban hubs like Blacktown and Dandenong should be dilapidated, badly designed and subject to the whims of capital. The result for many may be a life that is better than comparable experiences in the US or the UK – but it is hardly the good life when compared with some more expansive idea of what life could be.

People do talk about this when asked. During the election I spoke to hundreds of people in the sort of areas Latham is praising as a celebration of choice and self-fashioning, and what I found – and in line with the Mackay/Huntley qualitative surveys over recent decades – is a great sense people have that, in the words of Philip Larkin, "something is pushing them/to the side of their own lives." House prices are pushing people dozens of kilometres from their work, where they are paying off homes that still suck in a large slice of their income. Commuting, a form of unpaid labour, for two, three, even four hours a day drains them of energy and keeps them from their friends and family. Student debt – less onerous than in the US, but persistent – is often a drag on getting ahead. Medical care over time in health systems that are public, but have become capricious through under-investment, feels like a lottery, terrifying, especially where children are involved. Inflated charges by the massive cartel monopolies that run features of life that are now essential – communications and finance – wear people down and make them feel powerless.

But quite aside from the fact that people do talk about these things – and express great dissatisfaction with many particular aspects of their lives – is a simpler, material judgment that the good life must involve better than a sixty- to seventy-hour working week (including commuting), with extra hours created by poor amenities, often in circumstances of persistent debt.

The degree to which the population of a prosperous country has been persuaded that there is no alternative to this arrangement over the past decades is extraordinary. Throughout the twentieth century, up to the 1970s, the hours of the working week was pushed steadily downwards. Successive benefits were won – sick leave, extended, vacation, RDOs and that Australian special, long service leave. And then it all stopped. An attempt by the union movement to start a 35-hour-week campaign in the Fraser years was defeated, and when the Hawke-Keating government took over, collective union power was diluted to such an extent that such campaigns not only proved difficult, but a more atomised culture made their conception impossible. What was instituted by that historic turn was a society increasingly based on work, growth and debt – and one that, as a collective choice, had never been explicitly chosen or consented to by the populace. Hidden within it was a massive backward step – raising a family and owning a home on one income became impossible for many people (this backward shift was disguised by a positive event overlaying it: the full access of women to the workplace and careers, from the 1970s on. But this development should have resulted in a reduction of the working week for everyone, not a vast inflation of base costs). To choose another sort of life – more time-rich, focused more on relationships, education, simply living – is to choose precariousness. There is not much hinterland between the two.

Categorical changes in the way we live may partially arise from the market (Henry Ford pioneered the weekend, for example, as an incentive for workers to accept his inhumanly repetitive working conditions), but it is only by categorical public action that they are generalised. Any social democratic party worth its salt should be focused on reconstructing social and economic life so that genuine choices between real alternatives are possible.

That emphatically does not mean that cultural constraints should be imposed on people in a moralising fashion. Those who want to live high accumulation lifestyles should be able to (for as long as that remains possible and notwithstanding a deeper ethical debate as to whether anyone *should do so*). But a progressive party – one that wants to win a mass base for its own self-interest, while advancing an idea of the good life based on a full idea of the human – should be creating a society in which it is possible to live a life that is both modest and secure, with affordable home ownership, flexible time and ready access to education – both training and for its own sake – throughout the life-cycle.

Labor should renew itself, not by looking for this or that gimcrack formula by Chris Bowen, Kim Carr etc., but by understanding what it was always fighting for in the first place. The slogan inscribed on the eight-hour-day monument outside Trades Hall, Carlton – the first sustained and success-ful eight-hour-day campaign in the world – announces "eight hours labour, eight hours recreation, eight hours rest." The crucial term there is "recreation" – not *rek*-reation, indoor cricket and stretching, but re-creation. Those who struggled for free time, a life, understood that that meant a becoming again, a recovery of one's full humanity from the alienation of work and the animal needs of sleep. Becoming human, as a collective and universal project, is the golden thread running through the progressive tradition. To subsume that under a single notion of "growth" – growth which flows along the channels dictated by capital – is not only a shrivelled vision of the good life, but is to concede much of the political territory to the laissez-faire individualist right. Of course they will tend to win if Labor ensures that the ideas they represent dominate the public imagination of how life could be.

There is also more than a touch of parochialism about the argument. Latham obviously loves Western Sydney, its people, and Australia more broadly, and wants to do best by them. But what do they know of Toongabbie, who only Toongabbie know? He should up sticks for a year or two and spend some time in Denmark or Sweden, see a country where people have finished work and are out on the streets by 4 p.m., much of the day still free to them, where the mortgage does not loom large, where higher education is free for all and people thus return to it repeatedly, where 400-plus days paid parental leave and fully subsidised child care liberates women and takes pressure off the early years of child-raising, and where the aged and chronically ill receive a phalanx of specialised and continuing care – all this, together with a culture and an economy far more dynamic than Australia's. Then he should go to the US, and spend six months in Cleveland or Kansas City, somewhere average, and talk to the people who have one week's vacation a year, whose health insurance was – until Obamacare – tied to their jobs, who accept that chronic disease will mean personal bankruptcy, whose children will emerge from a college with a $120,000 debt for an essential but third-rate degree – and hear many of them say that they are happy, their lives are content, that government is too big. Have they too found the final form of their society?

To be honest, I don't how Latham doesn't come into contact with more of this dissatisfaction with the new Australian settlement. It's bloody everywhere. Denied expression on its own terms, it flows into other channels – the imaginary fears and fantasies projected onto the (very real) refugee problem, for example. I can't help but feel that he has allowed his own conditions of life to affect how he sees the world, without realising that this is occurring, and factoring it in. After all, Latham has the sort of life I'm describing as the good one. Thanks to parliamentary superannuation, he has the space to pursue his interests and passions, rather than being subject to the brute demands of the market.

Latham's master argument, or one of them – that Labor will never become once again the natural party of Australian government (as it was in the 1980s and into the 1990s) – unless it reorganises its structures, is well made. The new ideas won't flow unless the relationship between intra-party interests and ideas is transformed. Once that is underway, and ideas can flow, Labor needs to have some more expansive processes. The Hawke-Keating reconstruction was in part done by reaching out to many progressive traditions outside the party – from Eurocommunists, such as Laurie Carmichael, to centre-right social market theorists – and in the UK New Labour was rebooted by the think-tank Demos, formed out of a diverse group, once again including a fair slice of British Eurocommunist thinking. No coincidence that, as we folks say. Labor should avoid any notion of "rebranding" or looking for a new ideology to pick off the shelf. Its members should reflect on the unchanging core of its philosophy and how that will take on new forms in a society whose needs and desires are a century away from "frugal comfort." Should they not, they will remain in the named pews, singing from an old hymn-sheet, subject to the sermons and homilies of capital.

GUY RUNDLE is a writer-at-large for *Crikey* and author of the Quarterly Essay *The Opportunist: John Howard and the Triumph of Reaction*. His most recent book is *Got Zip! The Australian 2013 election live from the campaign trail*, with First Dog On The Moon.

NICHOLAS REECE

The Australian Labor Party finds itself at one of the lowest ebbs in its 120-year history. At the recent federal election the Labor government was thrown out of office in a thumping defeat. Following elections in South Australia and Tasmania, due in March 2014, Labor could find itself out of office nationally and in every state of Australia. The last time that occurred was forty-three years ago, in 1970.

Any organisation interested in its own survival must take this as a powerful portent of the need for change and renewal. The year 1970 represents a powerful case study for modern Labor, a party with a keen sense of its history. It was the electoral failure of this era that provided the impetus for major reform and modernisation. Under the leadership of Gough Whitlam and many others, the party ended its outdated narrow focus on nationalisation and industrial relations by developing a new agenda for education, health and urban services. It transformed itself from the party of "redistribution" to the party of "opportunity." It overhauled the antiquated union control of its structures and attracted thousands of new members from all walks of life. It reached out to new groups of voters, including rapidly growing numbers of white-collar workers. It tapped into emerging social movements like feminism and environmentalism. And it developed a vision for Australia's future. From these foundations Labor would enjoy four decades of (relative) electoral success at both federal and state levels.

Today modern Labor finds itself at something like a 1970 crossroads. If there is any good in the latest federal election defeat, it will come from the hard lessons the party must now learn. The logical response to defeat is to examine what went wrong and be willing to embrace the reform and renewal necessary to bring about future success. That is what would occur in a rational organisation. That is what would occur in most organisations that face the unrelenting pressure to generate profit. But political parties are very strange beasts, so there is no guarantee that the party of reform will be capable of reforming itself. However, the early signs are positive. It seems the ALP is finally ready to embrace change on a scale not seen since the great leap forward of the 1970 era.

Inspired by Mark Latham's essay, I have tried to undertake some hard thinking on the future for Labor. This includes some ideas on how to reposition Labor as a modern progressive party, increase its relevance to a broader constituency, update its party structures and develop some new policy directions. Perhaps it is my Victorian perspective on politics, but I believe Labor can recover from its electoral demise more quickly than many assume. The electorate is more volatile than ever and there remains a strong desire for progressive, commonsense solutions to the challenges of our times. But none of this will occur unless the party faces up to the reform task with the same honesty, purpose and courage that the likes of Gough Whitlam, John Button, Bob Hawke, John Cain, Neville Wran, Don Dunstan and many others displayed the last time Labor found itself at this point.

*

When Labor won the 2007 election, it did so with a primary vote of 43 per cent. When it was thrown out of office six years later, its primary vote was 33 per cent. It is not easy to lose 10 per cent of your primary vote across just two elections. This was more than just government disunity and a problematic campaign. It was also the result of deeper forces in the economy, society and party system that were working against Labor.

Labor's election defeat in September represented a new low point after two decades of decline in the party's vote. In the six elections of the Hawke-Keating era (1983–96), Labor's primary vote averaged 44 per cent. In the six elections since (1998–2013), Labor's primary vote has averaged just 38 per cent. By contrast the Coalition primary vote across the past six elections has averaged 43 per cent. With the exception of the 1998 One Nation/GST election, the Coalition's vote is less volatile than Labor's. There has been some attrition, but the Coalition primary vote remained higher than 40 per cent even when Rudd demolished Howard in 2007.

With the party having originated as the political wing of the labour movement, it is not surprising that Labor supporters have historically been blue-collar workers and trade unionists. However, these voting patterns have shifted over time with social and economic change. The Keating government's loss at the 1996 election saw the number of manual workers voting Labor fall below 50 per cent for the first time. In the almost twenty years since, this vote has remained historically low. The exception was the 2007 election where the Coalition's WorkChoices industrial relations policy featured. But by the 2010 election, it was on the decline again, down to 46 per cent. Early analysis of the 2013 election result suggests it has fallen further again.

The decline in support for Labor among blue-collar workers was offset by rising support among growing numbers of white-collar middle-class voters. These voters were attracted to Labor because of its support for quality-of-life issues in the 1970s and economic reform in the 1980s. At a state level, Labor also attracted young families in the growing suburbs of Australia with its support for the basics of health, education, transport and urban development.

But Australian voting behaviour continues to change with a further fragmenting of the electorate. A simple analogy helps make the point. In the 1960s most Australian households were either a Ford family or a Holden family. Today there are hundreds of car-makers and models in the market to cater for a diversity of consumer preferences and lifestyles. Australia's electoral laws strongly encourage a two-party system, so that Labor and the Coalition find themselves preserved in a Ford-versus-Holden type of struggle. But the task is much more complex now as they have to compete for support across a much more diverse range of voter groups with differing economic circumstances, lifestyles, social outlooks and household formations. So they need to have a product range – in this case the candidates, policies and vision – that speaks to a majority of this diverse electoral market.

The decline in Labor's primary vote shows it has not been successful in building the coalition of socio-economic groups needed to win an enduring electoral majority. It has struggled to craft an appeal to a broad enough segment of the electorate relative to the Coalition parties. Undoubtedly, it has a difficult balancing act between working-class and middle-class voters; those primarily interested in economic security and those with post-materialist values; voters in the outer suburbs and inner suburbs; socially conservative and socially progressive voters; and new migrant groups, established migrant groups and the established white working-class. The conservatives have become skilled at exploiting divisions among these groups. The emergence of the Greens as a left-of-centre party appealing to post-materialist voters has compounded the problem. This has left Labor confronted with the structural problem of losing votes to both the Coalition on its right and the Greens on its left.

*

The Australian Labor Party is not alone in these struggles. On the same weekend the ALP was defeated in Australia, the Norwegian Labour Party also lost office following a national election. These results are not surprising. Left-of-centre parties have become locked in a cycle of underperformance in advanced democracies. In 1999 all but two EU governments were controlled by social democratic parties. Today only ten out of twenty-eight member states have a centre-left government (in 2011 it was just five out of twenty-seven). Meanwhile, among Westminster democracies like Australia, Britain, Canada and New Zealand, centre-left parties all find themselves in opposition. There are, of course, some very notable exceptions: Barack Obama's (Democrat) win in the US presidential race in 2012, François Hollande's (Socialist) win in the French presidential race the same year and Enrico Letta's (Democratic Party) elevation to prime minister following elections in Italy in 2013. But the broad trend is strikingly clear.

Those who hoped the collapse of financial markets in 2009 would usher in the end of neoliberalism and restore support for traditional social democratic policies have been sorely disappointed. This then poses a fundamental question about the electoral appeal of left-of-centre parties in advanced democracies. Abstract theoretical debates on the left about a "paradigm shift" in Western capitalism in the aftermath of the global financial crisis have gained little traction. Meanwhile, the remedies of the right are simple and direct, casting the state as restrictive, wasteful and inefficient. More importantly, parties of the right have worked out how to appeal to the economic and social aspirations of the traditional working-class supporters of left-leaning parties.

Latham describes this phenomenon very well in his essay. While the electorate has become more fragmented, social surveys consistently show the number of people identifying themselves as "middle class" has increased to over 50 per cent. These households are typically aspirational, self-reliant and do not see as relevant the traditional prescriptions of the left involving heavy interference from the state or anyone else. They do not expect governments to control economic outcomes but rather to foster an environment in which they can advance themselves. Flexible and effective service delivery is all-important, and they do not care about the traditional delivery models that some in the left cling to as an article of faith.

Finally, right-of-centre parties in advanced democracies continue to use policy debates on immigration, crime and patriotism to win over working-class traditionalists and wedge centre-left parties between their middle-class progressive and working-class conservative voting bases. This tactic has become even more effective given the economic uncertainty following the global recession.

*

Does all this mean that centre-left politics is dead? Not at all. There remains a strong constituency for a progressive movement that addresses everyday concerns with commonsense solutions that create opportunity but also ensure fairness. Politics is more volatile and major-party loyalty is weaker than ever before. Notwithstanding all its troubles, federal Labor needs only a 5 per cent swing to be back in government. In Victoria, where state Labor maintained a reputation for strong and competent government, a disciplined Labor Opposition finds itself electorally in front on the latest opinion polls.

Labor should not be seduced into thinking it needs to radically reinvent itself as a working-class conservative party, a European-style social democratic party, a Liberal-lite party or even a Greens-lite party. Labor has a long and uniquely Australian history and ethos as the champion of the "fair go," the reformers, the nation-builders and the defender of the working man. But to make itself truly competitive again Labor will need to embrace a new wave of reform. Just as the scale of the electoral challenge is comparable to 1970, so too is the magnitude of the reform task.

*

In an increasingly diverse electorate, all major political parties face challenges holding together the alliance of voters necessary to form government. The Coalition faces its own set of challenges in balancing the interests of different constituent groups like big and small business, middle-class voters and working-class traditionalists, farmers, conservatives, liberals, free-market supporters and rent-seeking industries, long-standing Liberal voters and younger voters.

Historically, Australian political parties have shown themselves to be quite adept at identifying and reaching out to new constituencies. In the 1970s, as we have seen, Labor did this by using new policies and values to appeal to the rising middle-class, including professionals, educators and public servants. From the 1970s to the 1990s, Labor's support for multiculturalism and a belief in the "fair go" was used to win the support of new migrant groups.

For its part, the Liberals during the Howard era effectively used cultural debates to win support from working-class traditionalists. They also made major inroads among the fabled "tradies," those skilled tradesman turned independent contractors and small-business owners. The Liberals worked out that nowadays, tradies are more interested in tax laws than industrial relations and have a strong belief in reward for effort. More recently, the Liberals have tried to build support among new migrant voters, particularly in the Chinese and Indian communities, by welcoming their arrival in Australia, appealing to their entrepreneurial spirit and supporting traditional notions of the family.

Assembling a winning coalition and holding it is harder than ever. The achievement of the Obama campaign in the 2012 US presidential race in this is truly remarkable. By contrast, one of the reasons the Republican campaign failed was because it did not appeal to a broad enough cross-section of the changing American public. Labor needs to think deeply about its potential winning coalition of supporters, lest it fall into the same trap. Labor should not give up on its traditional working-class base, as some commentators have suggested. Nor should it walk away from its progressive supporters. Instead, Labor can straddle these groups if it gets better at communicating its values. Not in terms of sectional interests or the language of "class," but instead in terms of the "fair go," "opportunity" and belief in "community" and "support for services that families rely on."

There are a number of constituencies for which Labor is well placed to build its support. But to connect with them Labor needs to do the hard work of consultation, recruitment, policy and narrative development. Some of these groups include:

- *Aspirational families in the suburbs*: this remains a large and critical voter cohort that decides election results more than any other. While the socio-economic diversity of this group is increasing the number of people calling themselves "middle-class" is also on the rise. Labor needs to develop a new dialogue with these "modern families" that recognises their diversity as well as their aspirations and self-reliance. Labor can win the support of these families through its commitment to new education, health and transport services, provided it does not get hung up on old delivery models.

- *Small-business groups*: many small businesses find themselves facing unfair competition or monopolistic behaviour from big business – for example, franchise operators in shopping centres, suppliers of major supermarkets, or truck drivers and tradies who find themselves working as sub-contractors. Labor can assist these groups by standing against powerful interests and using policy tools like unfair contract laws. A progressive Labor Party also has a good cultural fit with small businesses in emerging industries like ICT, biotechnology, clean energy and cultural and personal services. Finally, many people work in small business because of the flexibility it offers them with their family life – this is something Labor should be able to tap into and improve upon.

- *Regional communities and farmers*: Labor should be able to build support off the back of its commitment to regional infrastructure like the NBN and other regional services. It should be prepared to stand up on behalf of farmers and regional businesses against larger vested interests. The success of regional independent candidates has shown the Coalition parties are vulnerable.

- *New migrant groups*: Labor should never shy away from its role as the representative of new migrants. Labor should recommit to helping new arrivals and building new communities.

To help reach these new constituencies Labor needs to think carefully about the people it chooses to represent the party. It needs to broaden the background and life experience of candidates so that they more truly reflect the diverse communities the modern party is seeking to represent. Organisational reform to open up candidate selection procedures is critical to achieve this.

*

Gough Whitlam's reforms to Labor's internal structures in the late 1960s helped usher in a modern era for the party. Whitlam democratised party conferences, increased the power of the parliamentary party at the expense of the extra-parliamentary wing and increased the power of the party leader relative to caucus. While the details of the reforms will be different, it is an approach that modern Labor would do well to emulate. The party founded on a radical democratic experiment needs to show it is still capable of democratic innovation. It cannot keep commissioning major reviews by party elders and then ignore the more challenging findings. A bit of experimentation and trial and error should be embraced.

Freedom of conscience for Labor MPs

With its collectivist approach to politics, Labor has historically placed significant constraints on its MPs by binding them to the party line. Under the pledge signed by all Labor MPs, they are bound to vote in accordance with a decision of caucus and the platform or face expulsion from the party. The non-Labor parties do not bind their MPs in this way and they are granted the ability to make their own decisions on how to vote in parliament.

With an increasingly diverse electorate there is a strong argument for Labor to review this antiquated arrangement. MPs should be given more scope to express their individual views on issues where a policy is shown to conflict directly with the interests of their electorate or their conscience. The decision to allow a conscience vote on same-sex marriage allowed the ALP to campaign on the issue without compromising the religious views of some MPs. In a similar way, a conscience vote on asylum-seeker policy would provide relief to some MPs and candidates. Another example of this new arrangement would be to allow a Labor MP who represents an area heavily reliant on manufacturing to vote with her conscience on a proposal to reduce tariff protection.

In Britain the use of whip rules gives Labour MPs more freedom to represent their electorate and cast an independent vote when in parliament. A similar model could work for Labor in Australia. In the modern media environment these differences of opinion would be portrayed as division and a lack of control by party leadership. But this is a small price to pay to help unshackle Labor MPs so they can represent the diversity of the Australian people and bring together the alliance of voters that Labor needs to be successful. It will also help counter the damaging perception that the party is controlled by unionists and backroom operatives.

Direct election of the leader

When my response to Mark Latham's Quarterly Essay was published back in April 2013, the first reform of the ALP I suggested was to give ordinary party members a direct vote for the leader of the party. As I researched this reform, I was struck by how widespread its operation had become and the positive benefit it has had on political parties that have adopted it. The decision of Kevin Rudd to introduce this reform in August 2013 is a very welcome one.

In the UK and Canada, which are Westminster parliamentary democracies like Australia, *all* the major parties now give rank-and-file members a say in choosing the leader. These changes mean these democracies do not have the revolving door of party leadership that is a feature of politics Down Under. Moreover, their political parties have membership figures the Australian parties can only dream of. In 2012 Canada's left-of-centre, trade union–supported New Democratic Party held a ballot of its members for the leadership. As part of the election campaign, the party signed up

45,000 new people and now has 130,000 members. The other major progressive political party in Canada is the Liberal Party. It registered 130,000 members and supporters to participate in a leadership ballot in April 2013.

The ALP should investigate allowing people to join the ALP during the leadership campaign period and still cast a vote. Based on the Canadian experience this would provide a huge boost to membership figures but would need to be balanced against concerns about vote stacking. A second potentially worthwhile reform is to give members of affiliated unions a vote for the party leader. Importantly, the vote would need to be cast by individual union members, not as a bloc vote by the union. In this way Labor might make itself more attractive to the 40 per cent of union members who do not vote for the ALP.

Primaries

Mark Latham's main proposal for party reform involves the introduction of community-based primary pre-selections that allow party members and registered "supporters" to vote for the local candidate. He argues that local primaries will attract new branch members and volunteers, pre-select better candidates, provide a valuable profile boost for the successful candidate for the election and transform the party's culture through community engagement.

As secretary of the ALP in Victoria, I was involved in Australia's first primary pre-selection, held in the outer metropolitan state seat of Kilsyth in 2010. The Kilsyth primary and subsequent primaries held in the Sydney mayoral race by the

ALP and in a NSW state seat by the Nationals have enjoyed modest success.

The accusation that primaries will give rise to "money politics and corruption" has not been evident in the trials to date. Opposition to primaries comes from vested interests in the ALP, who see them as a challenge to their power base. It also comes from those in the rank and file who see primaries as devaluing their own party membership by allowing "non-members" to vote in party elections. Nonetheless, community-based primaries have had enough success to warrant their further trial, including in a winnable parliamentary seat.

Labor and the unions

Trade unions are the largest and most representative community movements in Australia, looking after 2 million Australians and their families and campaigning for the interests of all workers. Unions provide manpower and financial resources that help the ALP at election time. The union movement also helps keep the party grounded in the concerns and values of ordinary working Australians.

Mark Latham argues stridently for a reduction in the power of the union movement within the ALP and believes it is the influence of unions through the factions that has created a destructive culture within the federal caucus. While I do not agree with all of Latham's reforms, I do agree it is time to recalibrate the relationship between the Labor Party and the trade union movement. It is simply not tenable to have affiliated unions that represent around 10 per cent of the workforce continuing to have 50 per cent of the vote in major forums in the ALP. (Union membership makes up 18 per cent of the workforce, but the two biggest unions in Australia represent teachers and nurses and neither of these is affiliated with the ALP, nor are a number of divisions of the public sector unions.)

The Australian Candidate Study for the 2007 election found that 83 per cent of Labor candidates said that they had been active in a trade union or staff association. This one statistic provides a powerful insight into the degree of control the union movement exercises over the party. Party reforms should open up the stranglehold that union-sponsored candidates have on ALP pre-selection processes, allowing people from other backgrounds to be pre-selected. This should be part of a broader range of measures that increases the role of party members in electing people to party forums and pre-selecting candidates. These changes should include lowering the percentage of delegates appointed by unions to key party forums, including those with a role in candidate selection. A further helpful reform would be to allow party members to directly vote for Senate candidates. This will help diversify Labor's parliamentary ranks and provide a further welcome democratic shot in the arm to the organisation.

People in the Labor Party like to think of themselves as being part of a movement, not just a political party. The party's origin in the trade union movement is obviously the reason for that sentiment. But in the modern era that founding spirit should now be extended to other groups. A further reform should allow non-union organisations, such as those in the NGO sector or groups like Rainbow Labor, to affiliate with the ALP with voting rights for members.

*

In continental Europe the parties of the left have come to the conclusion that they need to form progressive coalitions in order to hold government. The era of social democrat dominance is over, as greens and liberal-centrist parties have performed well among growing new constituencies. Meanwhile, in the US and UK, the major parties of the left have not formed a coalition with other parties of the left and, in the case of the US, face no major challenge from any other progressive party.

All of these advanced democracies share similar demographic changes, but their different voting systems produce these different electoral results. Australia's electoral laws put us somewhere between the US/UK and continental Europe, with preferential voting in single-member electorates in the lower house and proportional representation in multi-member electorates in the Senate. The electoral rules in the lower house strongly favour the continuation of the two-party system, but where we end up is still the subject of considerable speculation.

Three years ago it looked as if Australia might be heading down the European route of a progressive coalition. Now that appears less likely. One lesson from the Gillard government that everyone in Labor seems to agree on is that a coalition-type arrangement with the Greens must be avoided at almost all costs. The view of both the left and the right of the ALP towards the Greens has hardened considerably. The Greens are no longer seen, as they were previously in some quarters, as fellow travellers. Instead, they are seen as the enemy. This is because the Greens are viewed within Labor as cynically having claimed credit for everything Labor did that appealed to their supporters but, at the same time, attacking Labor for not doing enough. Second, the Greens' campaign efforts focus mostly on attacking Labor, because at the end of the day they are competing to win seats of sitting ALP members. Third, the result of this process is a diminution in Labor's primary vote with no guarantee of a flow through of Green preferences. This is unlike the relationship between the Liberal and National parties, where three-cornered contests and direct attacks on each other are avoided.

The electoral forces that may one day drive Labor and the Greens into a cooperative arrangement are in a state of flux. On the one hand, Labor's primary vote is down, making it more dependent than ever on Green preferences. On the other, the Greens are of less help electorally to Labor as their vote is also down as a consequence of the retirement of Bob Brown and the rise of other protest parties like the Palmer United Party. The loss of the balance of power voting-bloc in the lower house and Senate will also make it harder for the Greens party to remain relevant and may depress its vote further. Finally, while asylum-seeker policy remains a point of great contention, policy differences in other areas – such as carbon pricing, Tasmanian forestry, state funding for private schools and death duties – have narrowed.

So for the time being it appears the relationship between Labor and the Greens will remain a highly competitive one.

And it would appear to be in Labor's best interest that this is the case.

*

It seems that no article on the future of Labor is complete without a list of new policy ideas for the party to pursue. Mark Latham identified three policy areas that he believes are fertile policy ground for Labor: the next steps in the education revolution, the alleviation of poverty and the underclass, and responding to the challenge of climate change. In Chris Bowen's recent book I counted at least twenty significant new initiatives. Latham and Bowen are two of the genuine forward-thinkers in progressive politics in Australia and their suggestions deserve proper debate. Both of them have realised that the next wave of ALP policy must promote a new social and economic model that includes individual opportunity, choice and initiative while at the same time providing social services to an acceptable minimum standard.

I will add to this debate by simply identifying two ideas that I believe provide a fertile field for further progressive policy development. The first idea centres on the need for the state to do *more with less*. This requires some hard thinking on new models of public service delivery that will require the state to engage with new providers – public, private and voluntary – in new ways. This may include contracting, partnering, co-production, inter-governmental collaboration and volunteering. It is important for progressive thinkers to keep ahead of this trend and identify ways for the public sphere to improve services and outcomes for citizens by making full use of the alternative ways of getting things done. If they do not, then conservative politicians will end up controlling the agenda and this will result in the state doing *less with less*.

A second idea that has taken off among progressive thinkers in the UK is the concept of "predistribution." While David Miliband recently admitted that the term "does not fit on an electoral pledge card," it also provides a good framework for some new policy thinking. The basic idea is that because of the tendency of markets towards inequality and instability there needs to be action upstream in order to curb abuse of market power and empower citizens with rights, information and control. Instead of equalising through tax-and-spend or tax-and-transfer, policy-makers think more broadly about how to engineer markets to create fairer outcomes from the beginning. This can be achieved by equalising economic power through improving consumer and employee rights, better information disclosure, or by improving equality through improved educational attainment or workers access to childcare.

Finally, there are four specific areas where I think Labor can take a clear policy position that is different to the Coalition's, and where there is both a policy *and a political* opportunity.

Tackling climate change

During the 2013 election, the University of Melbourne in partnership with the University of Sydney and the ABC undertook Australia's largest ever social survey, Vote Compass. With 1.3 million responses, weighted using census data, we were able to get an accurate read on the views of Australian voters on the issues. The survey showed that 61 per cent of Australians want the government to do more to tackle climate change. Women and younger voters feel most strongly about taking action on climate change, while less than one-fifth of respondents believe the government should do less. The Coalition has failed to grasp this. The carbon price hurt Labor in part because it was a challenging reform, but mostly because of a perception about a breach of trust. The Vote Compass survey showed opinion reasonably evenly divided on the carbon price, which is actually a significant improvement in support since its introduction. Putting a price on carbon pollution remains the least costly and most effective way for Australia to cut its emissions. It is a policy that Labor must not walk away from. It is a policy that is eminently saleable, particularly when the disaster of the policy alternative becomes apparent.

Improving the operation of the mining tax

One policy area that is clearly challenging for the Coalition is the mining tax. The Vote Compass survey found almost 60 per cent of voters support the miners paying more tax, while just 10 per cent believe they should pay less. While the Coalition has promised to scrap the mining tax, more than one-third of its supporters believe miners should pay more tax. The Rudd and Gillard governments' handling of the mining tax was problematic from beginning to end. Properly argued and executed, the mining tax could be an improved source of revenue for the government. Commodity prices may have fallen and the growth rate of the Chinese economy may have slowed, but Australia is still about to enjoy the biggest increase in mining output in its history as the resources boom moves from the investment to the production phase. Surely a properly designed mining tax, not its abolition, can deliver massive benefits for the Australian public.

Building and funding infrastructure

Tony Abbott often says he wants to be an "infrastructure prime minister," but his anti-debt rhetoric and policy settings mean Australia is not even going to come close to meeting its infrastructure backlog. Meanwhile, a very big idea is taking hold among leading Australian policy-makers, economists, business executives, the labour movement and the superannuation sector. In essence, it involves a new cooperative approach to infrastructure investment in which government plays a much bigger role in the financing of projects, together with improved transparency and an independent assessment of productive returns. Suitable projects would then be privatised, providing a source of funds to be recycled for the next project, and opening up attractive investment opportunities for Australia's $1.6 trillion in superannuation savings. Under the plan the Commonwealth would take advantage of historically low interest rates and its strong balance sheet to debt-fund infrastructure projects that can be repaid by the states through their operating budgets or other means. The proposal is now being pushed in various forms by no fewer than five former or current Reserve Bank board members. Surely this is a policy idea worthy of Labor's nation-building tradition.

Building an innovation economy

As Australia moves from the investment phase to the production phase of the mining boom, policy-makers need to consider what will drive the next wave of economic growth. As outlined above, one answer is a step up in public infrastructure investment. A second is a renewed focus on building an innovation economy. Australian policy-makers remain far too timid in supporting innovation. The INSEAD Global Innovation Index for 2012 ranked Australia a lowly twenty-third – we rank well on innovation inputs, including research and skills, but weak on innovation outputs, such as new products and entrepreneurship. World leaders in innovation, such as the Nordics, Israel and Singapore, show that one of the keys to success is support for research as well as a generous system of tax or financial support for start-ups. With these sorts of policies, Nordic countries have been responsible for the recent emergence of new globally successful businesses such as Skype, Spotify and Rovio Entertainment, the maker of Angry Birds. Labor should become the champions of the relentless pursuit of innovation and productivity by business, encouraging a new entrepreneurial culture in Australia that recognises failure is often a step on the pathway to success.

*

In writing this piece I am conscious that I have added further pages to the national pastime of speculating on the future of the ALP. Much of this work is not helpful. Over and above all the ruminating and scribbling, the single best thing the

ALP could do for itself is to win an election. A victory in a significant election would help bring some perspective back to the forecasts of the demise for Australia's oldest and largest progressive political party. After all, it was just over five years ago that the ALP held government nationally and in every state and territory in Australia for the first time in its history.

For the Labor Party to be successful again, it must embrace renewal and reform on the same scale as it did back when it was at the 1970 crossroads. As Gough Whitlam said in this earlier era, the debate is about the party first, then the policies, and finally the people. Those reforms occurred only because of the courage and purpose shown by the great leaders of the party at that time. It remains to be seen whether the leaders of today's party are equal to the task.

NICHOLAS REECE has worked as the Victorian ALP secretary and a senior adviser to the prime minister, Julia Gillard, and to former Victorian state premiers Steve Bracks and John Brumby. He is now a public policy fellow at the University of Melbourne's Centre for Public Policy.